Cierra Block

NEW YORK
BLOCK by BLOCK

OH EDITIONS

To my family,
for the adventures we've had
that shaped how I see the world.

Cierra Block

NEW YORK
BLOCK by BLOCK

New York block by block

CONTENTS

PART ONE

New York by Food 9

PART TWO

New York by Locals 51

PART THREE

New York by Interest 101

PART FOUR

New York by Season 143

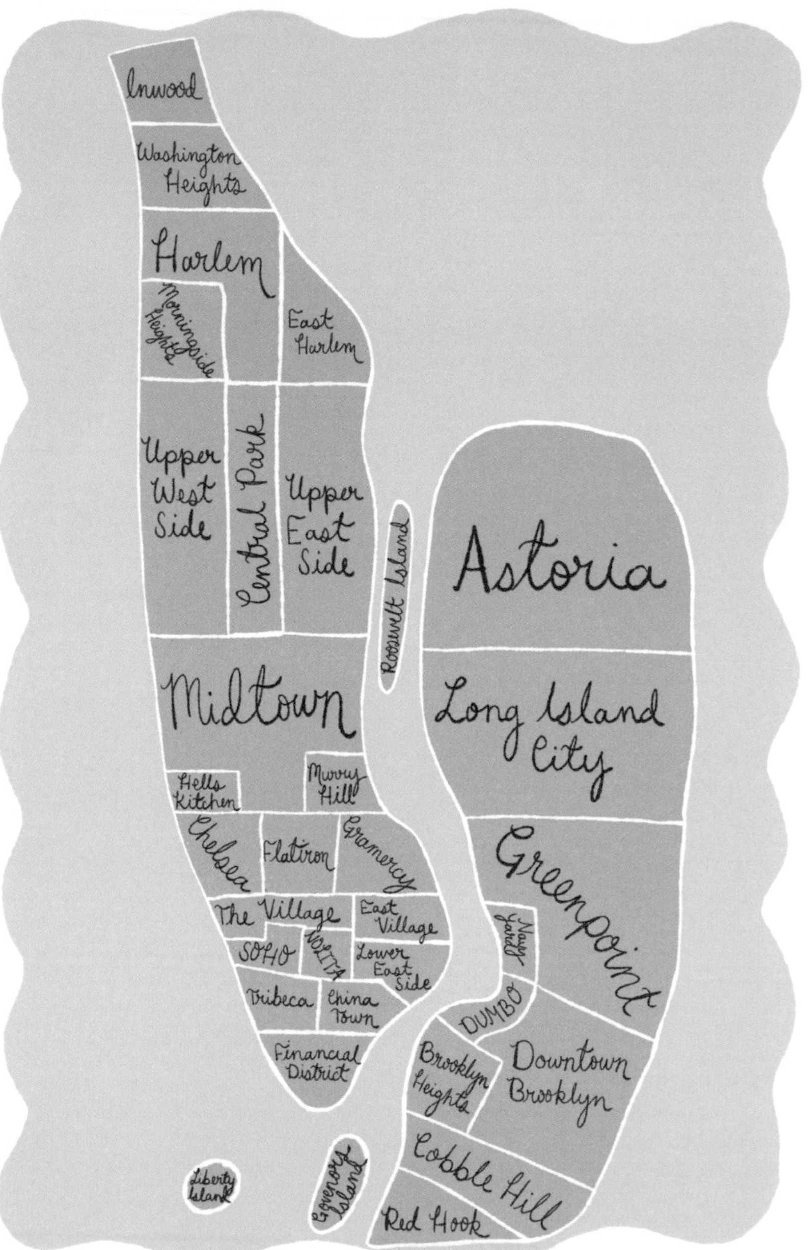

Inwood

Washington Heights

Harlem

Morningside Heights

East Harlem

Upper West Side

Central Park

Upper East Side

Roosevelt Island

Astoria

Midtown

Long Island City

Hells Kitchen

Murray Hill

Chelsea

Flatiron

Gramercy

Greenpoint

The Village

East Village

NOLITA

SOHO

Lower East Side

Navy Yard

Tribeca

China Town

DUMBO

Financial District

Brooklyn Heights

Downtown Brooklyn

Liberty Island

Governors Island

Cobble Hill

Red Hook

Travelling for me is a way to step away from the everyday and explore, discover, and experience life at a different pace. The best trips are the ones where you have unexpected experiences, where you leave space for wondering and allow yourself time to sit and take it all in.

My goal when creating these illustrated guides is to inspire your next adventure. I want you to use my guides to create memorable experience in one of the best cities in the world. Every map I create starts with an idea. It might be, Where are the best places for brunch? What are the places everyone should visit in Chelsea? Or, Where in New York can you lose hours browsing the shelves of a beautiful bookshop? I spend hours walking around neighbourhoods, sitting in coffee shops, perusing shops, trying new-to-me bakeries and cafes, and looking for hidden corners, looking for the best of the best.

Humans have been using maps for thousands of years. Maps help intuitively understand the relationship between where we are and where we want to go. And all the better if they lead you to a hidden corner of New York or a delicious bakery!

In this book, I hope you find some inspiration, whether it's your first visit, you're a seasoned vacationer or an all-your-life local. That's the wonderful thing about New York: there's always more to explore.

Cierra x

New York block by block

NEW YORK

BY FOOD

PART ONE

BAGELS + BAKERIES + COFFEE SHOPS + DESSERTS + BRUNCH

+ ICE CREAM + FOOD TRUCKS + FOOD MARKETS + DINERS + PIZZA

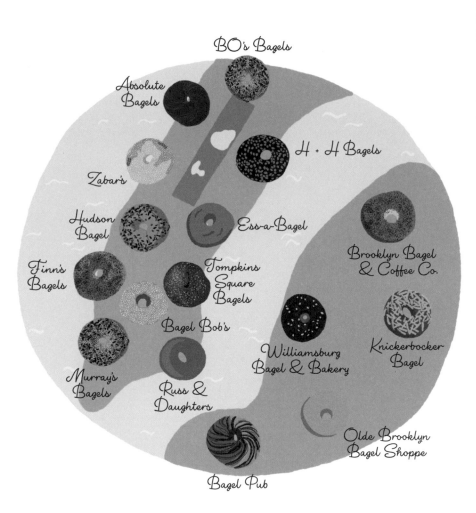

BO's Bagels

Absolute
Bagels

H + H Bagels

Zabar's

Hudson
Bagel

Ess-a-Bagel

Brooklyn Bagel
& Coffee Co.

Finn's
Bagels

Tompkins
Square
Bagels

Bagel Bob's

Knickerbocker
Bagel

Murray's
Bagels

Russ &
Daughters

Williamsburg
Bagel & Bakery

Olde Brooklyn
Bagel Shoppe

Bagel Pub

NYC BAGELS

NEW YORK BY FOOD

When you are in *New York City* there are a few foods you have to eat, and a bagel is one of them. Lightly *toasted* and served with a thick layer of *cream cheese,* there is no better breakfast in my opinion.

The history of the bagel has deep roots in NYC. It was first brought to the US by *Jewish immigrants* in the early 1900s. Fast-forward to today and they can be found in bakeries and delis on *every street* in the city. Deeply rooted in tradition, the process of making bagels has changed little since the turn of the century.

Most bagel shops have a *few seats,* but if the weather is nice, I'd plan to take it away and *enjoy it* on a park bench.

Absolute Bagels
2788 Broadway, Upper West Side, 10025
Delicious bagels served up with no frills. You can't go wrong with your order here, from flavoured cream cheese to a Nova (smoked salmon).

Bagel Bob's
Multiple locations, Greenwich Village, Upper East Side
Classic bagel shop with regular and mini bagels on offer.

Bagel Pub
Multiple locations, Brooklyn, Chelsea, West Village
An extensive menu serving up bagels as well as classic American breakfast food, sandwiches and burgers.

BO's Bagels
235 W 116th St, Harlem, 10026
The speciality bagel sandwiches here are noteworthy, from The Andrew to The Uptown.

Brooklyn Bagel & Coffee Company
Multiple locations, Brooklyn, Chelsea, Greenwich Village,
Perfectly chewy bagels served with intriguing cream cheese options.

Ess-a-Bagel
Multiple locations, Midtown, Gramercy, Dumbo
Extensive options when it comes to cream cheese and other bagel fillings.

Finn's Bagels
477 10th Ave, Midtown West, 10018
Bagels and sandwiches served with classic NYC fillings, from Nova to pastrami.

H&H Bagels
Multiple locations, Upper East Side, Upper West Side
Unfussy bagel shop serving up yummy bagels and sandwiches in classic combinations.

Hudson Bagel
691 9th Ave, Hell's Kitchen, 10036
Fresh bagels with an excellent array of cream cheeses to choose from.

Knickerbocker Bagel
367 Knickerbocker Ave, Brooklyn, 11237
Bagels, pancakes, sandwiches, soup, salad, this bagel shop
has something for everyone.

Murray's Bagels
500 6th Ave, Greenwich Village, 10011
Delicious speciality sandwiches alongside an array of classic
bagel combinations.

Olde Brooklyn Bagel Shoppe
645 Vanderbilt Ave, Brooklyn, 11238
Classic bagels with a great selection of cream cheese offerings.

Russ & Daughters
Multiple locations, Brooklyn, Hudson Yards, Lower East Side
A NYC institution. This four-generation, family-run business serves
up the best of the best when it comes to bagels and smoked fish.

Tompkins Square Bagels
Multiple locations, East Village
Offerings include classic bagel flavours and vegan options as well as a
French toast or chocolate-chip bagel for those with a sweet tooth.

Williamsburg Bagel & Bakery
73 Lee Ave, Brooklyn, 11211
Bagels and baked goods served fresh. Try their speciality crunchy
fried lox bagel if you are feeling indulgent.

Zabar's
2245 Broadway, Upper West Side, 10024
Pop into their takeaway cafe for their mouth-watering Nova bagel,
and take home a chocolate babka for good measure.

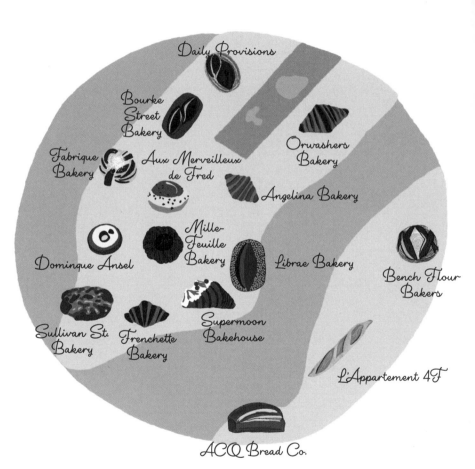

Daily Provisions

Bourke
Street
Bakery

Orwashers
Bakery

Fabrique
Bakery

Aux Merveilleux
de Fred

Angelina Bakery

Mille-
Feuille
Bakery

Librae Bakery

Bench Flour
Bakers

Dominque Ansel

Sullivan St.
Bakery

Frenchette
Bakery

Supermoon
Bakehouse

L'Appartement 4F

ACQ Bread Co.

NYC BAKERIES

NEW YORK BY FOOD

Bakeries in NYC represent the *diversity* of culture of the immigrants who helped *build the city* into what it is today, and there is no shortage of *selection*. From cinnamon buns to sourdough, croissants to Cronuts, you can find *artisan bakeries* in every neighbourhood of the city. So whether you are looking for a fresh loaf of *sourdough*, the perfect chocolate brioche or a freshly baked croissant, you are sure to find what you are looking for in these *amazing* bakeries.

ACQ Bread Co.
543 Clinton St #1, Brooklyn, 11231
Baking up delicious loaves and cookies. Definitely try the milk bread and treat yourself to a fermented rye chocolate cookie or two for the road.

Angelina Bakery
Multiple locations, Hell's Kitchen, Times Square
It will be tough to decide between stuffed croissants, Italian doughnuts, focaccia or a sandwich.

Aux Merveilleux de Fred
Multiple locations, Midtown, West Village
The NY outpost of this well-loved French bakery. Best to get two chocolate brioches so you can have one now and one later.

Bench Flour Bakers
43-18 25th Ave, Queens, 11103
Croissants, scones, and all sorts of delicious pastries are made from ingredients sourced from local NYC farmers.

Bourke Street Bakery
Multiple locations, Chelsea, Grand Central Terminal, NoMad, Upper West Side
This Aussie bakery offers up a great selection of baked goods from sausage rolls to lamingtons.

Daily Provisions
Multiple locations, Manhattan West, Union Square, Upper West Side, West Village
Start with a breakfast sandwich, everything croissant or a biscuit, but be sure to order a cruller or two as well.

Dominque Ansel
189 Spring St, SoHo, 10012
Worth the wait in the queue to get your hands on an original Cronut or any of the other delightful patisseries on offer here.

Fabrique Bakery

348 W 14th St, Meatpacking District, 10014
Cult Swedish bakery known for their cardamom and cinnamon buns,
this spot is cozy and fully of hygge.

Frenchette Bakery

220 Church St, Tribeca, 10013
Head inside the Merchants Square Building to find this lovely bakery.
Try the canelé or pistachio croissants if they haven't sold out.

L'Appartement 4F

115 Montague St, Brooklyn, 11201
A charming bakery serving up French pastries, delightful cookies,
and scrumptious baguettes.

Librae Bakery

35 Cooper Sq, NoHo, 10003
Airy bakery with a great selection of Middle Eastern-inspired pastries.
Try the babka, pistachio croissant and Jerusalem bagel.

Mille-Feuille Bakery

Multiple locations, Greenwich Village, Prospect Heights, Upper West Side
Try the chocolate brioche and the chocolate almond croissant, as well as
their namesake dessert, a classic mille-feuille.

Orwashers Bakery

Multiple locations, Upper West, Upper East Side, Roslyn Heights
Artisanal loaves and bagels are on offer here as well as a great
selection of sweet treats.

Sullivan St. Bakery

Multiple locations, Chelsea, Hell's Kitchen, SoHo
Italian-style bakery serving up loaves, pastries, focaccia and
bomboloni (filled doughnuts).

Supermoon Bakehouse

120 Rivington St, Lower East Side, 10002
Known for their stuffed croissants that are as lovely to look at as they are to eat.

Gertrude

Coffee Project New York

Culture Espresso

Variety Coffee Roasters

Drip Drop Cafe

La Cabra

Kinship Coffee

Stumptown Coffee Roasters

Homecoming

Interlude Coffee & Tea.

Mud

Alita

Alita Cafe

Black Fox Coffee Co.

Felix Roasting Co.

Brooklyn Roasting Company

Butler

Devoción

% Arabica

Ciao Gloria

COFFEE SHOPS

Coffee has been a New York *staple* since the Dutch began importing it in the 1600s. Initially it was seen as a luxury drink as it was time consuming to roast and brew. It wasn't until the early 1900s during NYC's industrial age that coffee became a drink for the masses. Italian and Greek migrants to the US brought their *love of coffee* and coffee traditions, expanding drink offerings to espressos, cappuccinos and endless diner refills.

These days you can find everything from artisan single-origin, small-batch coffee to flavoured drinks and other fancy concoctions. With cafes, coffee shops, and coffee carts on nearly *every street*, it really is no wonder that New Yorkers drink more *coffee* per capita than anywhere else in the USA.

% Arabica
20 Old Fulton St, Brooklyn, 11201
Passionate about the perfect coffee.

Alita Cafe
797 Grand St, Brooklyn, 11211
Roasting their own coffee and offering delectable pastries, made on site.

Black Fox Coffee Co.
Multiple locations, Financial District, Manhattan West, Midtown East
Gourmet coffee from some of the best roasters around the world.

Brooklyn Roasting Company
200 Flushing Ave, Brooklyn, 11205
Breakfast and brunch served alongside specialty coffee.

Butler
Multiple locations, Dumbo, SoHo, Williamsburg
Bespoke coffee and a seasonal menu serving up breakfast and lunch.

Ciao Gloria
550 Vanderbilt Ave, Brooklyn, 11238
Modern coffee and lovely meals on offer.

Coffee Project New York
Multiple locations, East Village, Chelsea, Midtown East, Brooklyn
Sustainability is just as important as taste at Coffee Project NY.

Culture Espresso
Multiple locations, Garment District, Midtown
Come for the coffee, stay for the chocolate-chip cookies.

Devoción
Multiple locations, Brooklyn, Flatiron District
Columbian coffee and fresh pastries served in an idyllic shop.

Drip Drop Cafe
107 Thompson St ST2, SoHo, 10012
Cozy coffee shop with coffee baked goods made to perfection.

Felix Roasting Co.

Multiple locations, NoHo, NoMad, SoHo

Beautiful ambiance, serving coffee alongside breakfast and lunch.

Gertrude

204 W 96th St, Upper West Side, 10025

Australian cafe serving quality coffee and quick bites.

Homecoming

Multiple locations in Brooklyn

A coffee/plant shop, where you can grab a coffee and a beautiful bouquet.

Interlude Coffee & Tea.

145 Hudson St, Tribeca, 10013

Coffee served alongside a great selection of house-baked pastries.

Kinship Coffee

Multiple locations in Brooklyn

Single origin coffee and baked goods served in a quaint environment.

La Cabra

152 2nd Ave, East Village, 10003

Delicious coffee and equally yummy Swedish-style cardamom bun.

Mud

307 E 9th St, East Village, 10003

Coffee and brunch by day and beers and wine by night.

Stumptown Coffee Roasters

Multiple locations, Ace Hotel, Brooklyn, Greenwich Village

Quaint coffee shop serving up house-roasted coffee and pastries.

Variety Coffee Roasters

Multiple locations, Bushwick, Chelsea, Greenpoint, UES, Williamsburg

This vintage feeling coffee shop is cozy and serves great coffee with a selection of mouth-watering baked goods.

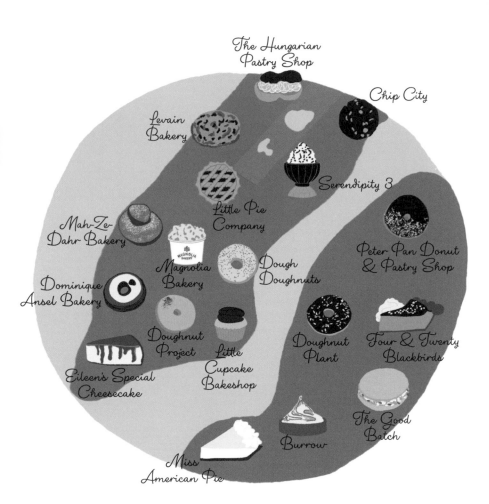

The Hungarian
Pastry Shop

Chip City

Levain
Bakery

Serendipity 3

Mah-Ze-
Dahr Bakery

Little Pie
Company

Peter Pan Donut
& Pastry Shop

Magnolia
Bakery

Dough
Doughnuts

Dominique
Ansel Bakery

Doughnut
Project

Doughnut
Plant

Four & Twenty
Blackbirds

Little
Cupcake
Bakeshop

Eileen's Special
Cheesecake

The Good
Batch

Burrow

Miss
American Pie

DESSERTS

New York has been the *birthplace* of many ubiquitous desserts. Cupcakes, cookies, *cheesecake*, doughnuts and more all had their humble beginnings in New York City. The Dutch brought doughnuts with them; a German immigrant created NYC-style cheesecake; and while cupcakes have been around for over 100 years, the way we enjoy them today is thanks to the NYC bakeries that made them popular in the early 2000s.

Bakers today are just as *adventurous* in creating new desserts – from the Cronut to birthday cake truffles, banana pudding to brioche doughnuts, NYC is a true *melting-pot* of desserts and no visit to the *Big Apple* is complete without sampling them.

Burrow
68 Jay St (back of the lobby at suite 119), Brooklyn, 11201
Everything is lovingly made and delicious here.

Chip City
Multiple locations, Brooklyn, Rockefeller Center, Upper East Side, Upper West Side, West Village
Big gooey New York-style cookies with a weekly changing menu.

Dominique Ansel Bakery
189 Spring St, SoHo, 10012
Try the OG Cronut and beautiful desserts.

Dough Doughnuts
Multiple locations, Downtown Brooklyn, Grand Central Terminal, Lower East Side, Queens, Williamsburg
Delicious doughnuts with classic and seasonal flavours on offer.

Doughnut Plant
Multiple locations, Downtown Brooklyn, Grand Central Terminal, Lower East Side, Williamsburg
Try the crème brûlée doughnut or the wonder wheel.

The Doughnut Project
10 Morton St, West Village, 10014
Unique doughnut flavours will make you want to keep coming back.

Eileen's Special Cheesecake
17 Cleveland Pl, Nolita, 10012
Darling cupcake-sized cheesecakes offered in a variety of flavours.

Four & Twenty Blackbirds
Multiple locations in Brooklyn
A local pie shop baking up classic home-made pies.

The Good Batch
936 Fulton St, Brooklyn, 11238
Enormous stuffed cookies, ice-cream sandwiches and delightful cakes.

The Hungarian Pastry Shop
1030 Amsterdam Ave, Upper West Side, 10025
Old-school pastry shop that has a loyal client base, many of whom are writers or students.

Levain Bakery
Multiple locations, NoHo, Williamsburg, Upper East Side, Upper West Side, Harlem, Wainscott
Mouth-watering cookies the size of your hand and worth the queue.

Little Cupcake Bakeshop
Multiple locations, Brooklyn and Nolita
Serving up classic American desserts such as cupcakes and more.

Little Pie Company
424 West 43 St, Midtown West, 10036
Darling mini pies served in over a dozen flavours.

Magnolia Bakery
Multiple locations across NYC
The banana pudding and cupcakes are a must-try.

Mah-Ze-Dahr Bakery
Mulitple locations, West Village and Midtown
Try the brioche doughnut, monkey bread or a scallion biscuit.

Miss American Pie
86 5th Ave, Brooklyn, 11217
Diner-style cafe serving up sweet and savoury pie by the slice.

Peter Pan Donut & Pastry Shop
727 Manhattan Ave, Brooklyn, 11222
Delicious doughnuts that are worth queueing up for. The sugar twist, sour cream cake doughnut and the honey dip are not to be missed.

Serendipity 3
225 E 60th St, Upper East Side, 10022
Known for their Frozen Hot Chocolate and quirky.

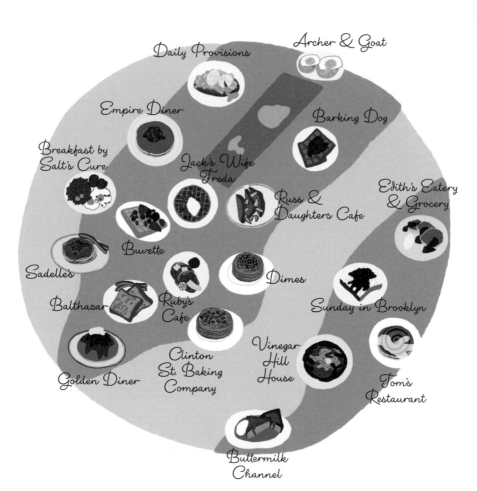

Daily Provisions

Archer & Goat

Empire Diner

Barking Dog

Breakfast by
Salt's Cure

Jack's Wife
Freda

Russ &
Daughters Cafe

Edith's Eatery
& Grocery

Buvette

Sadelle's

Dimes

Balthazar

Ruby's
Cafe

Sunday in Brooklyn

Golden Diner

Clinton
St. Baking
Company

Vinegar
Hill
House

Tom's
Restaurant

Buttermilk
Channel

BRUNCH

Brunch is one of the most *popular* meals in New York and it is no wonder why. Fresh stacks of pancakes, *perfectly cooked* eggs, French toast, avocado toast, waffles, bagels, not to mention the delicious drinks on offer. The NY *brunch scene* covers every type of brunch cuisine, so whether you are looking for an Aussie-inspired brunch packed with *fresh flavours*, a stack of American-style pancakes, or a *Middle Eastern*-inspired menu, you'll be sure to find something that hits the spot.

Archer & Goat
187 Malcolm X Blvd, Harlem, 10026
Known for their spiced French toast and hot chicken sandwich.

Balthazar
80 Spring St, SoHo, 10012
Traditional French cuisine is on offer for brunch here.

Barking Dog
Multiple locations, Hell's Kitchen, Upper East Side
Doggy friendly restaurant with all the classic brunch dishes
on offer.

Breakfast by Salt's Cure
27 1/2 Morton St, West Village, 10014
The oatmeal griddle cakes are divine at this quaint brunch spot.

Buttermilk Channel
524 Court St, Brooklyn, 11231
From buttermilk pancakes to scrambles, brunch here is divine.

Buvette
42 Grove Ct, West Village, 10014
French-inspired American brunch. Try the hot chocolate and the waffles.

Clinton St. Baking Company
4 Clinton St, Lower East Side, 10002
A great brunch spot with delicious chicken and waffles.

Daily Provisions
**Multiple locations, Manhattan West, Union Square,
Upper West Side, West Village**
Delicious breakfast sandwiches and old-fashioned cinnamon
crullers that often sell out, so get them if you can.

Dimes
49 Canal St, Lower East Side, 10002
California-style brunch menu with tacos and açaí bowls.

Edith's Eatery & Grocery
312 Leonard St, Brooklyn, 11211
Twists on Jewish staples. From savoury brunch to challah French toast.

Empire Diner
210 10th Ave, Chelsea, 10011
Upscale diner with retro vibes that offers up a great brunch.

Golden Diner
123 Madison St, Lower East Side, 10002
Brunch dishes inspired by New York's diverse food culture.

Jack's Wife Freda
Multiple locations, Chelsea, SoHo, West Village, Williamsburg
A wonderful spot offering up a delicious American-Mediterranean brunch.

Ruby's Cafe
Multiple locations, East Village, Murray Hill, SoHo
An Aussie-inspired cafe serving fresh and vibrant breakfast dishes.

Russ & Daughters Cafe
Multiple locations, Brooklyn, Hudson Yards, Lower East Side
Offering NYC breakfast staples of bagels, latkes and smoked fish.

Sadelle's
463 W Broadway, SoHo, 10012
Known for the bagels and salmon, this SoHo spot is a favourite for brunch.

Sunday in Brooklyn
348 Wythe Ave, Brooklyn, 11249
The pancakes here are worth the wait.

Tom's Restaurant
2880 Broadway, Harlem, 10025
Serving up all the classic diner foods in this iconic restaurant.

Vinegar Hill House
72 Hudson Ave, Brooklyn, 11201
Wonderful atmosphere to enjoy a seasonal brunch.

The New York Icery

Caffé Panna

Anita La
Mamma del
Gelato

Seed +
Mill

Soft
Swerve

Taiyaki

Ample Hills
Creamery

Cones

Mikey
Likes It

Sundaes
& Cones

Il Laboratorio
del Gelato

Milk Bar

Milk &
Cream Cereal
Bar

Chinatown
Ice Cream
Factory

Malai
Ice Cream

Sugar Hill
Creamery

Brooklyn
Farmacy &
Soda Fountain

NYC ICE CREAM

NEW YORK BY FOOD

New York's notoriously *warm summers* make ice cream almost a necessity to *keep cool*. If you are looking for something more adventurous than your local Mister Softee, you are thankfully *spoilt for choice*. From *soft serve* to *gelato*, *Italian ice* to *milkshakes*, your choices of great ice cream spots is *nearly endless*.

Ample Hills Creamery
Multiple locations, Chelsea, Brooklyn, Astoria, Upper West Side, Financial District
Playful flavours based on America's favourite desserts, from peppermint patty to the munchies, this tasty ice cream will make you smile.

Anita La Mamma del Gelato
Multiple locations, Upper East Side, NoMad
A huge array a flavours to suit every palate.

Brooklyn Farmacy & Soda Fountain
513 Henry St, Brooklyn, 11231
A 1920s pharmacy turned ice cream parlour.

Caffè Panna
77 Irving Pl, Gramercy Park, 10003
A curated assortment of flavours on offer.

Cones
272 Bleecker St, West Village, 10014
A great assortment of ice cream and sorbet flavours.

Il Laboratorio del Gelato
188 Ludlow St, Lower East Side, 10002
Churning up gelato in almost every flavour you could imagine.
Let your tastebuds go wild trying unique flavours.

Malai Ice Cream
268 Smith St, Brooklyn, 11231
South Asian-inspired ice cream with spiced blended in: lemon cardamon, orange fennel and spiced peanut crunch to just name a few.

Mikey Likes It
199 Ave A, East Village, 10009
Fun flavours with names that will put a smile on your face.

Milk & Cream Cereal Bar

159 Mott St, Lower Manhatten, 10013

Step back into your childhood with cereal-topped ice cream.

Milk Bar

Multiple locations, Upper West Side, Nomad, Williamsburg, Nolita, East Village, West Village, Midtown

Pop in for the famous cereal milk ice cream soft serve or cake truffles.

Seed + Mill

409 W 15th St, Chelsea, 10011

Tahini Soft Serve is the only ice cream on the menu here but it is amazing. Go for the sundae, which is drizzled with more tahini and sprinkled with halva.

Soft Swerve

Multiple locations, Lower Manhattan, Lower East Side, Kips Bay, Flushing

Asian-inspired soft serve (think purple yam and black sesame).

Sugar Hill Creamery

Multiple locations, Central Harlem, West Harlem, Brooklyn

Classic flavours with a twist are served alongside seasonal favourites.

Sundaes and Cones

95 E 10th St, East Village, 10003

A great selection of classic and unique flavours of ice cream.

Taiyaki NYC

Multiple locations, Chinatown, Williamsburg

Japanese soft serve enjoyed in a taiyaki fish cone.

The New York Icery

Multiple locations, Upper West Side, Brooklyn Heights

Naturally vegan Italian ice served in a variety of fresh flavours.

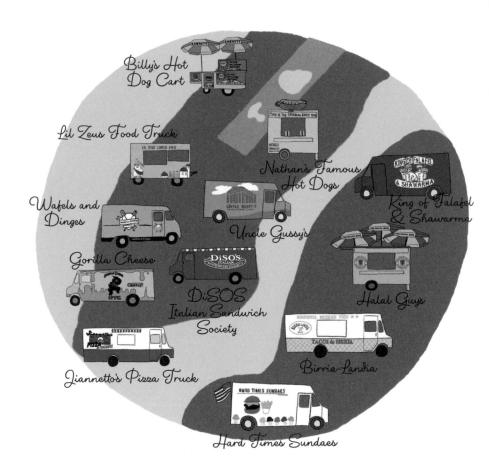

Billy's Hot
Dog Cart

Lil Zeus Food Truck

Nathan's Famous
Hot Dogs

King of Falafel
& Shawarma

Wafels and
Dinges

Uncle Gussy's

Gorilla Cheese

DiSOS
Italian Sandwich
Society

Halal Guys

Birria-Landia

Jiannetto's Pizza Truck

Hard Times Sundaes

FOOD TRUCKS

NEW YORK BY FOOD

NYC's food cart scene has been around since the early 1800s, when "OG" food *vendors* would sell peanuts or oysters. As more people from around the globe began to call NYC home, they brought their food, *culture and traditions* with them and added to the melting pot of food on offer throughout the city.

Even though food carts and trucks have *evolved over time*, their purpose stays the same: they are a quick and inexpensive way for people to eat. Today those living or visiting NYC are spoiled for choice when it comes to the *global range* of street food on offer. While you might have to queue up for some of the most popular food trucks, the lines always move quickly, and you'll be happy you waited once you've *enjoyed* the delicious food.

Billy's Hot Dog Cart

327 Central Park West #63, Upper West Side, 10025

Not all hot dog carts are created equal, and Billy whips up delicious dogs. Loaded with your toppings of choice, you can have a great meal from an iconic street cart.

Birria-Landia

Multiple locations, Queen's, Brooklyn, Bronx

A small menu that packs a big punch, and everything is delicious. The tacos and tostadas are a favourite, but their shop is great as well.

DiSO'S Italian Sandwich Society

Multiple locations – check their website

Two sandwich trucks that serve Italian deli-style subs, you can check their website for the locations. The sandwiches are named after famous Italian-Americans, and you can't go wrong with ordering The Fonz, Lefty Louie or The Godfather.

Gorilla Cheese

Multiple locations – check their website for that week's locations

A variety of cheese melts and sandwiches are on the menu. You can pick your favourite cheese for your sandwich, and be sure to get a side of tater tots.

Halal Guys

W 53rd St & 6th Ave, Midtown, 10019

Serving up flavourful halal chicken and falafel platters and wraps in large portions. These guys are the original halal food cart.

Hard Times Sundaes

1017 Cortelyou Rd, Brooklyn, 11218

Unpretentious burgers and milkshakes crafted to perfection. You can't go wrong with their signature burger and the black-and-white milkshake.

Giannetto's Pizza Truck

90 Front St, Dumbo, 10043

Freshly baked pizza with a great sauce, served up quickly, makes this a great option for a quick bite.

King of Falafel & Shawarma
3015 Broadway, Queens, 11106
Generous portions of falafel and shawarma served as a platter or in a pita.
If you can't decide what sounds best, go for the shawafel.

Lil Zeus Food Truck
112 W 50th St, Midtown West, 10020
Chicken souvlaki pita and platters, as well as burgers, are on offer here.
A great spot to go when you want a quick fix of delicious Greek food.

Uncle Gussy's
345 Park Ave, Midtown, 10154
Greek-style pitas, platters, salads and burgers served fresh. Don't worry
if the queue is long as it moves quickly and food is prepared fast.

Wafels and Dinges
East Village, Midtown, Central Park
Belgian-style waffles with a variety of sweet topping options.
The perfect place to stop for a sweet treat!

Nathan's Famous Hot Dogs
787 5th Ave, Upper East Side, 10022
Hot dogs served in the traditional way with no
frills. You can opt for sauerkraut or onions, as
well as your choice of ketchup and mustard.

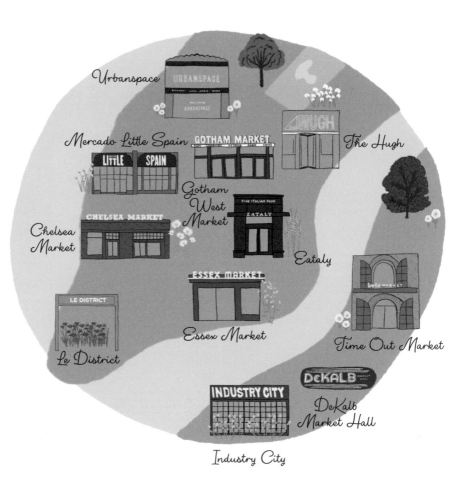

Urbanspace

Mercado Little Spain

GOTHAM MARKET

The Hugh

Gotham West Market

Chelsea Market

Eataly

Essex Market

Time Out Market

Le District

DeKalb Market Hall

Industry City

FOOD MARKETS

Markets have been a *central* part of NYC since its inception, and these market halls have lived many lives. *Chelsea Market* was originally a biscuit factory, The Time Out Market located in *Empire Stores* was originally a shipping warehouse that would have stored the likes of sugar and coffee, and Industry City was a *manufacturing* and distribution hub that was essential when New York was a major international seaport. These Markets now play host to a thriving food scene with *local vendors* and restaurants setting up shop to share a huge variety of food. A visit to these markets embraces the *history* of NYC while spotlighting the current food scene.

Chelsea Market
75 9th Ave, Chelsea, 10011
A vibrant market full of shops and restaurants and a fun place to explore with lots of food options. The perfect place to pop into for a quick bite after walking the High Line.

DeKalb Market Hall
445 Albee Sq W, Brooklyn, 11201
Dozens of local food vendors offering up classic NYC bites. With options including pastrami sandwiches, tacos, crepes and ice cream, a visit to this market will leave you happy and full.

Eataly
Multiple locations, Flatiron, Downtown
This Italian food hall has the best of the best when it comes to Italian dining and delicatessens. From take-away to sit-down restaurants, you'll find all sorts of Italian delights.

Essex Market
88 Essex St, Lower East Side, 10002
This Lower East Side market is full of great vendors offering up delicious eats. Hosting a collection of unique shops, cafes and restaurants, there is something for everyone.

Gotham West Market
600 11th Ave, Midtown West, 10036
Hell's Kitchen's own little market has a handful of restaurants offering up a good variety of food. From ramen to sushi and pizza to burgers, you are sure to find something that tastes delicious.

The Hugh
601 Lexington Ave, Midtown, 10022
Fifteen bars and restaurants are spread across this airy food hall. From lobster rolls and pizza to a gastro pub and artisanal bakery, you'll be sure to find something to enjoy any time of the day.

Industry City
220 36th St, Brooklyn, 11232
Great restaurants, cool shops, lovely food market . . . there is nothing not to love about Industry City. It is a vibrant place to wander around and has lots of great corners to discover.

Mercado Little Spain
10 Hudson Yards, Chelsea, 10001
This market features food and drink from all around Spain. From empanadas to tapas, paella to jamon, you'll find an excellent variety of restaurants serving up classic dishes.

Time Out Market
55 Water St, Brooklyn, 11201
This market in Dumbo boasts amazing views, great food and an energetic atmosphere. Enjoy a drink on the rooftop while watching the sunset over the Manhattan skyline.

Urbanspace
Multiple locations, Midtown, Midtown West
With a few locations dotted across Midtown, these food halls offer up a dozen or so delicious options and are a great place to go for a quick lunch or dinner.

Le District
225 Liberty St, Lower Manhattan, 10281
A spacious French food hall in Battery Park with beautiful views of the Hudson River, delicious restaurants and tempting patisseries, it feels like a trip to France and is a great place to visit.

Tom's Restaurant

TOM'S RESTAURANT

Old John's Luncheonette

Old John's

Lexington Candy Shop

Lexington Candy Shop LUNCHEONETTE

times square DINER & GRILL

Times Square Diner

BEL AIRE DINER

Bel Aire Diner

Empire Diner

EMPIRE DINER

JOE JUNIOR RESTAURANT
ALL BEEF BURGERS

Joe Junior

WAVERLY DINER   BREAKFAST LUNCH DINNER

Waverly Diner

PEARL DINER

JOHNY'S GRILL & LUNCHEONETTE
BREAKFAST • LUNCH

Johny's Luncheonette

DINER
DINER

Mike's COFFEE SHOP

Pearl Diner

Mike's Coffee Shop

CLARK'S RESTAURANT

SUNSET PARK DINER & DONUTS

Sunset Park Diner & Donuts

Clark's Restaurant

DINERS

Diners used to be a *staple* of every neighbourhood
in NYC; it was where workers could grab a quick
breakfast, lunch or dinner. While most of the diners
and *luncheonettes* are long gone, some of these
classic diners remain. Some have been restored
or reimagined, and a select few have remained *in
business for decades*, offering up *classic diner*
food with little fanfare or fuss.

Bel Aire Diner
31-91 21st St, Queens, 11106

This diner has an extensive menu, with classic diner food as well as Greek staples. Grab a booth and enjoy perusing the menu while you try to decide what to order.

Clark's Restaurant
Brooklyn Heights, 80 Clark St, Brooklyn, 11201

From pancakes and waffles to sandwiches and burgers, there is no shortage of options here. After your meal, enjoy a walk around the charming neighbourhood.

DINER
85 Broadway, Brooklyn, 11249

New American-style diner with a great atmosphere. Housed in a converted railcar, it is a great place for weekend brunch or lunch and dinner during the week.

Empire Diner
210 10th Ave, Chelsea, 10011

An upscale diner with a chic vibe. Breakfast is served until 4pm and the lunch and dinner menu is full of classics. My advice? Start with the buttermilk biscuits.

Joe Junior
167 3rd Ave, Gramercy Park, 10003

A true retro diner that will make you feel like you are in a New York from yesteryear. The food is your standard diner fare, with breakfast, sandwiches, burgers and more.

Johny's Luncheonette
124 W 25th St, Chelsea, 10001

This small but charming diner is open for breakfast and lunch, offering all your classic diner options from breakfast platters to sandwiches.

Lexington Candy Shop
1226 Lexington Ave, Upper East Side, 10028

Don't let the name fool you – this isn't a candy shop but offers up delicious diner food. One of the few remaining diners from the 1920s, the atmosphere is charming and they offer a great selection of milkshakes and handmade sodas.

Mike's Coffee Shop

328 DeKalb Ave, Brooklyn, 11205

An old-fashioned diner with the food to match. Eggs, waffles, burgers, sandwiches and more . . . you'll find all your favourite diner foods on offer here.

Old John's Luncheonette

148 W 67th St, Lincoln Sq, 10023

A neighbourhood diner with a vintage feel. Be sure to save room for dessert as their pies are a must-try!

Pearl Diner

212 Pearl St, Financial District, 10038

A classic diner that has changed little since it opened in the 1960s. There are no bells or whistles here but the variety and quality of food is great.

SUNSET PARK
DINER & DONUTS

Sunset Park Diner & Donuts

889 5th Ave, Brooklyn, 11232

This 24-hour diner serves up homemade doughnuts and sandwiches alongside breakfast favourites.

times square
DINER & GRILL

Times Square Diner

807 8th Ave, Midtown, 10019

Nostalgic atmosphere and great diner food in the heart of Midtown. Breakfast is served all day and the portions are large.

Tom's Restaurant

2880 Broadway, Upper West Side, 10025

This iconic diner was the inspiration for the diner in the TV show *Seinfeld*, but it hasn't let fame get it the way of good food and a great atmosphere.

WAVERLY   BREAKFAST
DINER   LUNCH   DINNER

Waverly Diner

385 6th Ave, Greenwich Village, 10014

Grab a booth and browse the extensive menu. Enjoy breakfast, lunch or dinner at this local favourite that stays open late.

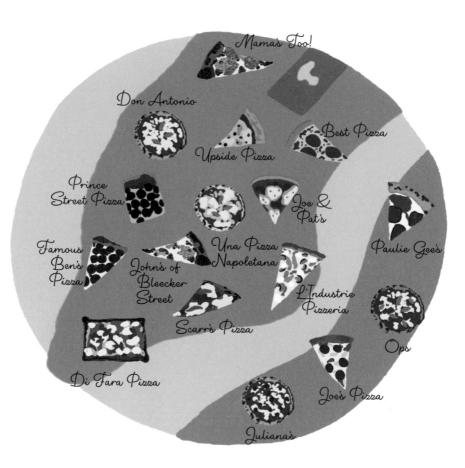

Mama's Too!

Don Antonio

Best Pizza

Upside Pizza

Prince
Street Pizza

Joe &
Pat's

Famous
Ben's
Pizza

Una Pizza
Napoletana

Paulie Gee's

John's of
Bleecker
Street

L'Industrie
Pizzeria

Scarr's Pizza

Ops

Di Fara Pizza

Joe's Pizza

Juliana's

NYC PIZZA

While *pizza* was invented in Italy, it definitely came into its own in New York City. The first NYC-style pizza shop opened in the early 1900s, but it wasn't until the middle of the century that it *became a staple* part of a New Yorker's diet. Before then it was enjoyed by the *Italian community* and seen by others as a foreign food. Nowadays every neighbourhood has more than a handful of pizza places worth visiting. It makes it quite the challenge to narrow it down to *the best*, but here are some of my favourites that are *worth travelling* to or do something a bit different.

Best Pizza

33 Havemeyer St, Brooklyn, 11211

Wood-fired pizza place offering up both regular and square slices.

Di Fara Pizza

1424 Ave J, Brooklyn, 11230

A NYC institution with no frills, just good pizza served by the slice or as a whole pie.

Don Antonio

309 W 50th St, Midtown, 10019

Neapolitan pizza served alongside inventive cocktails and beers.

Famous Ben's Pizza

177 Spring St, SoHo, 10012

Pizza served with no fuss or frills, but it's so, so delicious.

Joe & Pat's

168 1st Ave, East Village, 10009

An institution since 1960. The Tri-Pie is great, but you also can't go wrong with the Original.

Joe's Pizza

Multiple locations, Greenwich Village, Gramery, Lower Manhatten, Williamsburg

New York-style pizza at its best. Thin crust, tasty toppings and quick service.

John's of Bleecker Street

278 Bleecker St, Greenwich Village, 10014

Brick-oven pizzas baked to order with a grunge, hole-in-the-wall atmosphere that really adds to the whole experience.

Juliana's

19 Old Fulton St, Brooklyn, 11201

New York-style coal-fired pizza with all the classic toppings available. Go for the meatballs as a starter.

L'Industrie Pizzeria
254 S 2nd St, Brooklyn, 11211
Gourmet pizza with creative flavours. Try the Fig Jam and the New Yorker.

Mama's Too!
2750 Broadway, Upper East Side, 10025
If you are looking for something a bit more unusual, the gourmet pizzas here are top notch. Try the Poached Pear, Funghi or the Angry Nonna.

Ops
346 Himrod St, Brooklyn, 11237
An eclectic and unpretentious restaurant serving wood-fired sourdough pizza.

Paulie Gee's
60 Greenpoint Ave, Brooklyn, 11222
Retro vibes and delicious pizza. A perfect combo.

Prince Street Pizza
27 Prince St A, Nolita, 10012
The pepperoni is popular for a reason, but the Prince Perfection is great as well.

Scarr's Pizza
22 Orchard St, Lower East Side, 10002
Classic NYC-style pizza served with a retro atmosphere.

Una Pizza Napoletana
175 Orchard St, Lower East Side, 10002
Delicious Napoletana-style wood-fired pizza. Only open a few days a week, but they do take reservations.

Upside Pizza
Multiple locations, Greenpoint, Midtown East, Nolita, Garment District
Sourdough-based pizza with classic toppings on offer. Try the mushroom with lemon creme sauce, or go classic with their cheese or pepperoni pies.

NEW YORK

BY LOCALS

PART TWO

CHELSEA + GREENWICH VILLAGE + SOHO & NOLITA + EAST VILLAGE
/ LOWER EAST SIDE + MIDTOWN + UPPER WEST SIDE + UPPER EAST SIDE
+ FINANCIAL DISTRICT + WILLIAMSBURG + BROOKLYN HEIGHTS
+ CENTRAL PARK + ROOSEVELT ISLAND

A Hug From The Art World

Art Galleries

The High Line

EMPIRE DINER

Empire Diner

192 Books

Citizens of Chelsea

Intelligentsia Coffee

Billy's Bakery

CHELSEA MARKET

Chelsea Market

THE RUBIN MUSEUM OF ART

Rubin Museum of Art

Little Island Pier

Fabrique

CHELSEA

Chelsea is a great place to explore for both visitors and locals. It is full of art galleries, restaurants, quiet residential streets, museums and has one of the *most popular* walking paths in the city, the High Line. So, whether you are hitting up Chelsea Market and Little Island, doing a *gallery stroll* on a Thursday night or walking the High Line while enjoying the *beautiful views* and lovely art, there are countless ways you can enjoy this *vibrant* area of New York City.

Art Galleries

All over Chelsea

Chelsea is full of art galleries with ever-rotating exhibitions. From W 19th to W 26th Street, just west of 10th Avenue, you will find countless galleries featuring every type of art. Some favourites are Lisson Gallery, Hauser and Wirth, Agora Art Gallery and Andrea Rosen. On Thursday evenings the neighbourhood livens up with dozens of galleries staying open late for Gallery Night, a unique and fun way to see a lot of art while sipping a nice drink.

192 Books

192 10th Ave, 10011

This bookshop offers a well-curated selection of books, and lovely staff who are able to offer up great suggestions.

Billy's Bakery

184 9th Ave, 10011

A charming bakery feels like it was plucked out of a movie. Serving cupcakes, cookies, cheesecakes, pudding and more.

Chelsea Market

75 9th Ave, 10011

A wonderful food market with some great eateries. For Mexican, try Los Taco's #1 or Pia. Stop by Filaga for delicious pizza. For desserts, Seed + Mill have the best halva and out-of-this-world tahini ice cream, or opt for Doughnuttery, which sells freshly baked tiny doughnuts.

Citizens of Chelsea

401 W 25th St, 10001

This light and airy restaurant serves up breakfast and lunch with an Aussie twist. For something sweet, try the Banana Bread French Toast; for savoury you can't go wrong with the Cheddar Biscuit Sandwich.

Empire Diner
210 10th Ave, 10011

This upscale diner is a few steps above your typical greasy spoon. With art deco decor and high-quality food, a meal here won't disappoint.

Fabrique
348 W 14th St, 10014

This Swedish bakery has the most delicious Scandi-style cinnamon and cardamom buns, as well as incredible rye bread and tasty drinks.

The High Line
From W 30th St to West 13th St, 10011

This mile-and-a-half-long elevated walking park is a popular destination for a reason. With lovely views, interesting art, nice places to sit and lovely greenery, this pedestrian-only walkway is a great way to see Chelsea.

Intelligentsia Coffee
180 10th Ave at W 20th St, 10011

Located in the lobby of The High Line Hotel, this cafe serves up great coffee in a charming setting. A great place to meet with friends or relax after walking the High Line.

Little Island Pier
55 in Hudson River Park, 10014

Completed in 2021, this pier has been turned into a beautiful green space. With spectacular views, it's a great place to watch the sunset over the Hudson.

Rubin Museum of Art
150 W 17th St, 10011

Open Thursday through Sunday, the Rubin is home to a wonderful collection of artwork from Bhutan and the surrounding areas. On Friday night they have free admissions and a DJ, you just need to book in advance.

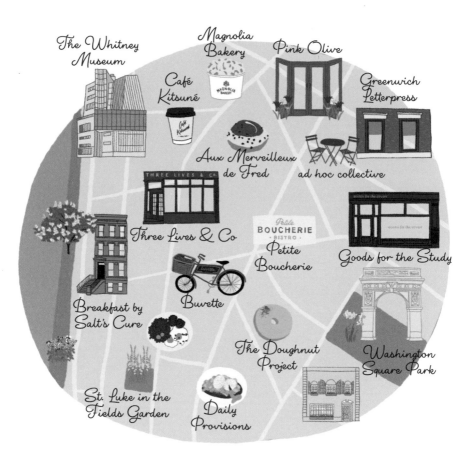

The Whitney Museum

Magnolia Bakery

Pink Olive

Café Kitsuné

Greenwich Letterpress

Aux Merveilleux de Fred

ad hoc collective

Three Lives & Co

Petite Boucherie

Goods for the Study

Breakfast by Salt's Cure

Buvette

The Doughnut Project

Washington Square Park

St. Luke in the Fields Garden

Daily Provisions

GREENWICH VILLAGE

NEW YORK BY LOCALS

Greenwich Village is a neighbourhood you can *never tire* of exploring. With an abundance of French-style bistros, quaint streets, lovely shops and *hidden corners*, the vibrant atmosphere here is always a *joy to experience*. Some of the best bakeries in NY are located here and you could easily *wile away* your day eating one *delicious treat* after the other. There is endless charm to be found in the *architecture*, as well as lots of great places to sit for a coffee and *people-watch*.

ad hoc collective
13 Christopher St, 10014
Head down the small flight of stairs to find this cosy cafe.

Aux Merveilleux de Fred
37 8th Ave, 10014
The West Village outpost of this beloved French bakery, serving up the best chocolate brioche and delicious meringue bites.

Breakfast by Salt's Cure
27 1/2 Morton St, 10014
The griddle cakes here are worth the visit alone. The small menu packs a punch, and everything is cooked to perfection.

Buvette
42 Grove St, 10014
With French-bistro vibes and serving breakfast favourites with a French twist, it's no wonder it is popular.

Café Kitsuné
550 Hudson St, 10014
Serving up great drinks and delicious pastries, this coffee shop is the perfect place to stop for a little pick-me-up.

Daily Provisions
29 Bedford St, 10014
A great cafe to pop into for breakfast or lunch. Try the everything croissant, seasonally flavoured crullers or a great assortment of sandwiches.

The Doughnut Project
10 Morton St, 10014
This doughnut shop is a must-visit when you are in Greenwich. Open Wednesday through Sunday, they often sell out by midday.

Goods for the Study
50 W 8th St, 10011
Inviting store with greetings cards, notebooks, a wonderful selection of pens in every colour and anything else you might need in your office.

Greenwich Letterpress
15 Christopher St, 10014

Cosy stationery shop with a large assortment of cards, notebooks and small gifts.

Magnolia Bakery
401 Bleecker St, 10014

A must-visit: this bakery serves some of New York's most iconic desserts, from delicious cupcakes to banana pudding.

Petite Boucherie
14 Christopher St, 10014

Little sister to the popular Boucherie restaurants, this quaint cafe serves classic French fare in surroundings that make you feel like you are in Europe.

Pink Olive
30 Charles St, 10014

Delightful home goods and stationery shop with lots of fun gifts.

St. Luke in the Fields Garden
485 Hudson St, 10014

This tranquil garden is a wonderful place to escape the hustle of the city.

Three Lives & Co
154 W 10th St, 10014

This compact bookshop packs in a lot. It is wonderfully curated and full of delightful books; it is hard to leave empty-handed.

Washington Square Park
Washington Square, 10012

A great place for people-watching and resting your feet. If the dosa food cart is there, queue up for one – you won't regret it!

The Whitney Museum
99 Gansevoort St, 10014

This large modern art museum has a wonderful collection as well as stunning skyline views.

Sweet Rehab

L'Appartement Sézane

Prince Street Pizza

Fountain House + Body

Vesuvio Bakery

McNally Jackson Books

Elizabeth Street Garden

Color Factory NYC

Dominique Ansel Bakery

Little Cupcake Bakeshop

Flipper's

MarieBelle

Little Moony

Egg Shop

SOHO & NOLITA

One of New York's *most popular* shopping destinations, SoHo is packed with boutiques, restaurants, cafes and bakeries. You can find everything from *luxury goods* to more affordable shops, and it is a lovely place to wander around. There are *ample cafes* to stop at as well, which are great for people-watching or catching up with a friend. This popular area with its *cobbled streets* can get quite crowded, so if you are heading here for a meal booking in advance is highly recommended.

Color Factory NYC
251 Spring St, 10013

This photo-worthy art exhibit encourages touching and has a giant ball pit at the end. A unique experience and fun for kids and adults of every age.

Dominique Ansel Bakery
189 Spring St, 10012

Home of the original Cronut, the popularity of Dominique Ansel hasn't waned since the bakery opened. A must-visit bakery for incredible desserts.

Egg Shop
151 Elizabeth St, 10012

This bright and airy cafe offers up a delicious selection of egg-centred breakfast and lunch dishes. Be sure to get a side order of mini doughnuts or buttermilk biscuits with honey butter.

Elizabeth Street Garden
Elizabeth St, 10012

This small community garden is packed with unique sculptures and is a great place to sit and relax, offering an often-needed reprieve from the hustle and bustle of New York.

Flipper's
337 W Broadway, 10013

The New York outpost of the OG Japanese soufflé pancake restaurant, offering up the fluffiest pancakes you can imagine with delectable toppings.

Fountain House + Body
105 Thompson St, 10012

Eco-conscious at its core, this shop has great sustainable supplies for your home and for yourself.

L'Appartement Sézane
254 Elizabeth St, 10012

A lovely shop with beautifully designed French clothing. From cheerful knits to lovely bags and shoes, browsing the clothes here is a delight.

Little Cupcake Bakeshop
30 Prince St, 10012

The charming facade on this shop draws you right in, and the excellent selection of puddings, cheesecakes and cupcakes makes your mouth water.

Little Moony
230 Mulberry St, 10012

A delightful children's shop that, despite its small size, has an amazing assortment of clothes, toys and gifts.

MarieBelle
484 Broome St, 10013

The Cacao Bar here has a decadent menu featuring hot cocoa, afternoon tea and pastries. Try the molten lava cake or their signature hot cocoa.

McNally Jackson Books
52 Prince St, 10012

A wonderful bookshop to quietly mosey through, with an expansive selection of books on every topic you can imagine.

Prince Street Pizza
27 Prince St, 10012

This takeaway pizza joint is perfect for a quick bite of delicious NY-style pizza. The pepperoni is a firm favourite, and the inevitable queue will move quite quickly, making it worth the wait.

Sweet Rehab
135 Sullivan St, 10012

Enjoy delicious French desserts in a beautiful cafe that is open late into the evening. From tarts to eclairs, you won't be disappointed.

Vesuvio Bakery
160 Prince St, 10012

Beloved Italian bakery serving fresh bread, bombolini, cookies, treats and sandwiches.

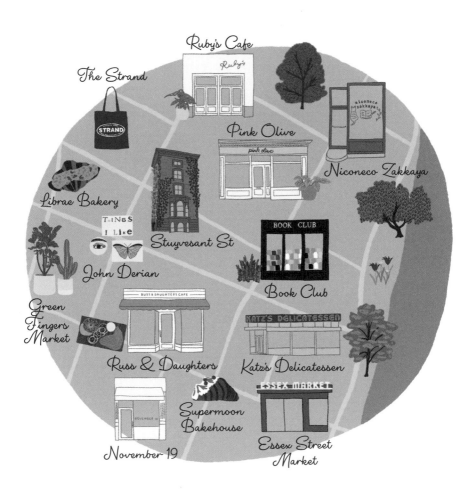

Ruby's Cafe

The Strand

Pink Olive

Niconeco Zakkaya

Librae Bakery

Stuyvesant St

John Derian

Book Club

Green
Fingers
Market

Russ & Daughters

Katz's Delicatessen

Supermoon
Bakehouse

November 19

Essex Street
Market

EAST VILLAGE / LOWER EAST SIDE

One of the landing grounds for early immigrants, the Lower East Side has seen wave after wave of *cultures* transform its streets and shops. Gentrification over the past few decades has changed the area and some old establishments have had to *reinvent themselves,* such as the newly renovated Essex Street Market, a *vibrant food* hall with food from around the world, whereas some shops have maintained their place in the community. Russ & Daughters and Katz Deli have been in operation for over a *hundred years* and remain *beloved* anchors of the community and its history.

Book Club
197 E 3rd St, 10009
Part book club, part coffee shop and part bar, this is a great place to
sit and enjoy a drink and a book.

Essex Street Market
88 Essex St, 10002
This indoor market is full of delicious eateries and food stalls. With a huge
variety of food, it is a great place to wander through and try new things.

Green Fingers Market
5 Rivington St, 10002
This charming plant shop is filled floor to ceiling with beautiful
greenery. With a huge assortment of plants, you'll be hard pressed
to go home empty-handed.

John Derian
6 E 2nd St, 10003
Whimsical and unusual goods fill this homewares shop. You are sure to
find something unique amongst the treasures here.

Katz's Delicatessen
205 E Houston St, 10002
Famous for its pastrami sandwich, this deli has been operating since 1888.
It's a popular place so be prepared to queue.

Librae Bakery
35 Cooper Sq, 10003
Middle Eastern–inspired baked goods with babka, tahini chocolate
cookies, beautiful rose pistachio croissants and much more.

Niconeco Zakkaya
263 E 10th St, 10009
This small Japanese stationery and gift shop is full of delightful treasures.
You'll find a unique collection of office goods and amazing stamps.

November 19
37 Orchard St, 10002

This homewares and gift shop is full of one-of-a-kind artisanal goods.
These unique items are thoughtfully displayed and a joy to peruse.

Pink Olive
439 E 9th St, 10009

A charming shop with a well-curated selection of children's clothes
and toys as well as beautiful cards, stationery and gifts.

Ruby's Cafe
198 E 11th St, 10003

Australian-style cafe serving up fresh flavours and all-day breakfast.
The Sweetcorn Fritters, Ricotta Hotcakes and Passionfruit Yoghurt are
all delicious; it will be hard to choose!

Russ & Daughters
127 Orchard St, 10002

Supplying New Yorkers with bagels and lox for over 100 years, this is the
perfect place to go for brunch. With freshly baked bagels, perfectly cured
salmon and tangy cream cheese, you can't go wrong.

The Strand
828 Broadway, 10003

One of the city's most-beloved bookstores. Selling new and used books,
you can easily wile away an hour or two perusing the shelves.

Stuyvesant St
E 10th St & Stuyvesant St, 10003

There is a small memorial park on this street offering a beautiful view
of the corner home that is covered in vines and has wisteria blooming
in springtime.

Supermoon Bakehouse
120 Rivington St, 10002

Open Thursday through Sunday, this bakery specialises in cruffins and
filled croissants in a variety of unique and delicious flavour combinations.

La Grande Boucherie

Beard Papa's

Burger Joint

Bibble and Sip

Joe's Home of Soup Dumplings

St Patrick's Cathedral

MoMA Design Store

The Meatball Shop

New York Public Library

The Morgan Library and Museum

Bryant Park

United Nations

Angelina Paris

Lady M Cake Boutique

Empire State Building

MIDTOWN

Midtown is one of the busiest places in NYC. With the Theatre District, Garment District, dozens of office buildings and some of the *busiest* train stations in the city, it can be overwhelming. However, amongst the hustle and bustle there are some *amazing* places to explore. From charming pastry shops to hidden burger joints, there are some great places to check out when you need a *reprieve* from shopping on 5th Avenue or a break from the Rockefeller Center crowds.

Angelina Paris
Bryant Park, 1050 6th Ave, 10018
A bit of Paris in the heart of New York. The hot chocolate is a must,
and all the desserts are created to perfection.

Beard Papa's
239 E 53rd St, 10022
At this cream puff bakery you can pick your own flavour combinations.

Bibble and Sip
253 W 51st St, 10019
Serving up amazing cream puffs and cakes that are almost too adorable
to eat, this bakery also has great drinks and savoury snacks.

Bryant Park
W 40th and 5th Ave,10018
A lovely place to sit and escape from the hustle and bustle of Midtown.

Burger Joint
119 W 56th St, 10019
Hidden in the lobby of Thompson Hotel is a hole-in-the-wall
burger bar. Serving up burgers and fries with no fuss.

Empire State Building
20 W 34th St, 10001
This art-deco skyscraper has an amazing history and is a wonderful place
to see the NYC skyline. Be sure to book tickets in advance.

Joe's Home of Soup Dumplings
7 E 48th St, 10017
The place to get delicious soup dumplings, as well as tasty Chinese food.

La Grande Boucherie
145 W 53rd St, 10019
Serving up classic French dishes from morning to night, as well as a
great pre-theatre menu, this is guaranteed to be a memorable evening.

Lady M Cake Boutique
36 W 40th St, 10018

Known for their mille crepe cakes, this cafe has a great assortment of different flavours. Everything always looks delicious, so best to take a friend and try a few flavours.

The Meatball Shop
798 9th Ave, 10019

Mouth-watering meatballs served in a variety of ways, from subs to pasta and salads to flatbreads, there is something for everyone.

MoMA Design Store
11 W 53rd St, 10019

Not surprising that the MoMA has one of the best gift shops; this is a great place to pick up a souvenir that you will enjoy for years to come.

The Morgan Library and Museum
225 Madison Ave, 10016

A wonderful museum with an absolutely stunning library. This museum is full of treasures and is well worth exploring.

New York Public Library
476 5th Ave, 10018

An iconic building that is just as beautiful inside as out. Be sure to wander through the library's Treasures exhibition.

St Patrick's Cathedral
E 50th and 5th Ave, 10022

This gothic cathedral, built in 1879, stands out against the high rises of Midtown. Free to explore; it is a great place to get a reprieve from 5th Avenue.

United Nations
405 E 42nd St, 10017

Take a guided tour of this impressive facility boasting architecture, artworks and murals from around the world.

Barney Greengrass

Broad Nosh Bagels

Janie's Baked Goods

Jacob's Pickles

Riverside Park

Zabar's

Délice Macarons

The Strand

American Museum of Natural History

Levain Bakery

Lincoln Center

Imagine Mosaic

UPPER WEST SIDE

Sandwiched between Riverside Park and Central Park, the Upper West Side has a *vibrant food scene*. With restaurants and bakeries lining Amsterdam Avenue and Broadway, there are seemingly *limitless options* when it comes to finding something delicious to eat. The neighbourhood itself is quite relaxed, with lots of large apartment complexes – such as the Apthorp, the San Remo and the Dakota – filling the skyline, as well as *charming streets* lined with brownstones. As you head south towards Columbus Circle you will find more and *more shopping options*, and if you head north you'll find Columbia University and St. John the Divine Cathedral – one of the largest in the world.

American Museum of Natural History
200 Central Park West, 10024
Popular with kids and adults alike, the Museum of Natural History is full of treasures. You can see a 15-ton meteorite, wander through the dinosaur exhibit or enjoy a space show, and so much more.

Barney Greengrass
541 Amsterdam Ave, 10024
A visit here is like stepping back in time. Since opening in 1908 this deli has had great breakfast options, especially if you are a fan of smoked fish. Be sure to order some latkes to share; you won't regret it.

Broad Nosh Bagels
2350 Broadway, 10024
This no-frills deli is a great place to grab a quick bite. An "everything" bagel toasted with scallion (spring onion) cream cheese is a classic order, but everything is delicious.

Délice Macarons
321 Amsterdam Ave, 10023
This French patisserie serves up all the classic French desserts and pastries. From macarons in every flavour to perfectly baked pain au chocolat, you can't go wrong with what you order here.

Jacob's Pickles
509 Amsterdam Ave, 10024
This restaurant is a popular place with locals and visitors. Serving up Southern-style comfort food, it is a great place to visit for brunch or dinner.

Imagine Mosaic
Terrace Dr, 10023
Located in Strawberry Fields, the garden and mosaic were created as a memorial to John Lennon after his death.

Janie's Life-Changing Baked Goods

212 W 80th St, 10024

This small bakery is serving up delicious pie-crust cookies.
The combination of cookie and pie crust with filling in between
makes for a unique and delicious treat.

Levain Bakery

167 W 74th St, 10023

These are THE cookies to eat in New York. Huge, chewy, delicious . . .
there is nothing quite like them. You can't go wrong on flavour choice,
so go with whatever speaks to you.

Lincoln Center for the Performing Arts

Lincoln Center Plaza, 10023

Home to the Met Opera and NYC Ballet, the Lincoln Centre is a
prime location to experience the arts. Check out their programme
to see if anything catches your eye.

The Strand

450 Columbus Ave, 10024

The Upper West Side outpost of this iconic bookstore is fun to putter
through. With a wonderful selection of books for adults and kids alike,
it is a must-visit if you are in the area.

Riverside Park

From 72nd to 158th St along the Hudson River

This four-mile-long park is one of the most stunning riverside parks
in NYC. With lovely playgrounds, running tracks, tennis courts and miles
of walking paths, this park is a wonderful place to ramble through.

Zabar's

2245 Broadway, 10024

Since 1934 Zabar's has been supplying New Yorkers with smoked fish
and high-quality groceries. For groceries head to the shop, but if you are
looking for takeaway their cafe has delicious sandwiches and bagels. The
Classic Nova is a must for salmon lovers, and don't leave without a few
slices of babka.

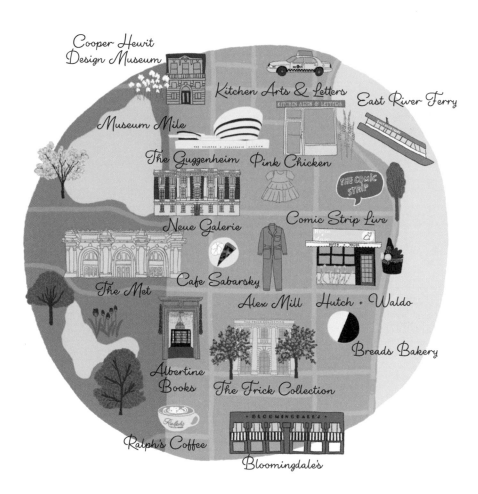

Cooper Hewit Design Museum

Kitchen Arts & Letters

East River Ferry

Museum Mile

The Guggenheim

Pink Chicken

Neue Galerie

Comic Strip Live

The Met

Cafe Sabarsky

Alex Mill

Hutch + Waldo

Breads Bakery

Albertine Books

The Frick Collection

Ralph's Coffee

Bloomingdale's

UPPER EAST SIDE

High-end shopping, world-class museums, Gilded-age mansions and a mixture of old-meets-new architecture makes the Upper East Side a *wonderful place* to explore. For those who enjoy retail therapy, a walk down Madison Avenue is a delight. Dotted with *designer stores* as well as local brands, there is no shortage of shops to inspire. If museums are more your thing the Upper East Side packs a punch with a group of *amazing museums* located in the "museum mile". From newer art at the Guggenheim to ancient ruins at the Met, there is something for all to enjoy. Among the museums and shops there are lots of *delicious places* to stop for a coffee or a bite to eat, rounding out a lovely a day in the UES.

Albertine Books
972 5th Ave, 10075

This bookstore features books in French and English, as well as books written by French authors, translated into English. Even if French isn't your thing, the bookstore is stunning and a true delight to walk through.

Alex Mill
1182 Madison Ave, 10028

The New York-based store features timeless casual wear for men and women. With classic designs and colours, anything you buy here will be sure to be a favourite for a long time.

Bloomingdale's
59th St and Lexington Ave, 10022

New York is home to several iconic department stores, and for over 100 years Bloomingdale's has had a flagship department store on this site. Selling clothes, homewares, accessories and more, wandering through here is wandering through history.

Breads Bakery
1294 3rd Ave, 10021

Baking up all manner of deliciousness, be sure to try their babka and black-and-white cookie.

Cafe Sabarsky
1048 5th Ave, 10028

Located in the Neue Galerie, this old-world Viennese cafe serves up delicious food in an equally amazing location. The traditional Austrian menu has delicious options from breakfast to dinner, but be sure to save room for dessert.

Comic Strip Live
1568 2nd Ave, 10028

This comedy club is the place to go for stand-up comedy. This intimate venue puts you right there with the comics and there are shows nearly every night.

East River Ferry

Ferry Dock, East 90th St, 10028

From East 90th Street all the way down to Wall Street, the East River Ferry offers up great views of Manhattan from the Upper East Side to the Financial District.

Hutch + Waldo

247 E 81st St, 10028

Serving breakfast and lunch, this laidback Aussie cafe offers up delicious food and drinks with a wonderful ambiance.

Kitchen Arts & Letters

1435 Lexington Ave, 10128

This bookstore's sole focus is books about food and drink; you will be sure to find inspiration among the shelves.

Museum Mile

Fifth Ave from 82nd St to 105th St

This mile-long stretch is home to some incredible museums. You have the Frick Collection, featuring European art; The Met, which houses artwork and treasures from the ancient world to contemporary designs; the Neue Galerie, with its collection of German and Austrian Art; the Guggenheim, showcasing contemporary art and designed by Frank Lloyd Wright; and the Cooper Hewit Design Museum, with extensive collections exploring different aspects of design.

Ralph's Coffee

888 Madison Ave, 10021

Located just inside the Ralph Lauren store is this stylish coffee shop, the perfect place to take a break after hitting the shops on Madison Avenue.

Pink Chicken

1198 Madison Ave, 10128

This charming children's clothing shop features fun prints, bright colours and easy-to-wear looks for boys and girls.

Eataly

FINE ITALIAN FOOD

EATALY

The National
September 11
Memorial &
Museum

Bowne &
Co., Stationers

BOWNE & Cº STATIONERS.

McNally
Jackson Books

McNALLY JACKSON BOOKS

Ellis
Island

Funny Face
Bakery

Museum of
Jewish Heritage

FRAUNCES
TAVERN

The Seaport

Liberty Island

Fraunces Tavern

The Battery

FINANCIAL DISTRICT

This historic quarter of New York City has been a *bustling area* ever since the first European settlers arrived on its shores. Where Old World meets New, with buildings that are almost as old as the country itself and *modern skyscrapers*, it really is a wonderful area to explore. Enjoy beautiful views along the Battery Park Esplanade, shop and dine in a *historic fishing* wharf or discover one of the many memorials and museums dotted through this area. From the Museum of Jewish Heritage to the 9/11 Memorial, there are many places to *stop* and pause for thought.

The Battery

Battery Park, 10004

This park at the southern end of Manhattan has beautiful tree-lined walkways with views of the harbour and Statue of Liberty. Sculptures and memorials punctuate the park and there are countless benches to sit on and enjoy the view. Enjoy the walk on the esplanade from Liberty Street all the way to the Whitehall ferry terminal.

Bowne & Co., Stationers

211 Water St, 10038

Established in 1775, this vintage print shop has a wonderful selection of letterpress cards, prints and stationery. For unique cards and local history, you can't do better.

Eataly NYC Downtown

101 Liberty St 3rd Floor, 10007

This Italian market is a great place to stop for lunch, dinner, a quick coffee or gelato. With a handful of restaurants and cafes, there are lots of great options when it comes to finding something delicious to eat.

Fraunces Tavern

54 Pearl St, 10004

Established in 1762, this tavern is the oldest restaurant in New York and is steeped in history. With good food and drinks, it is a great place to come and be immersed in history.

Funny Face Bakery

6 Fulton St, 10038

Baking up delicious NY-style chocolate chip cookies as well as quirky hand-decorated biscuits.

Liberty Island and Ellis Island

Visiting this iconic New York landmark is something that you should do at least once. If you book online, you can get access to climb up to the crown inside the statue. Ellis Island Museum reflects on its part in the history of immigrants to the United States.

McNally Jackson Books

4 Fulton St, 10038

Wonderful bookshop that embraces the history of the building.
Spread over two floors, it is the perfect place to browse.

Museum of Jewish Heritage

36 Battery Pl, 10280

This museum focuses on the history and stories from the Holocaust and
has changing exhibitions throughout the year. The museum is also home
to Lox Cafe, a great place to stop for old-world Jewish delights.

The Seaport

19 Fulton St, 10038

Formerly a fishing wharf, The Seaport has been beautifully restored
and is now home to many restaurants, cafes and shops.

September 11 Memorial & Museum

180 Greenwich St, 10007

The museum offers a dignified and respectful
memorial to a horrific day. The memorial outside
marks where the towers stood, with the names of
those who lost their lives that day.

Homecoming

Catbird

Bakeri

Donut Plant?

Beam

Everlane

Quimby's
Bookstore

Domino
Park

Gelateria
Gentile

Nick + Sons
Bakery

The Attic
Brooklyn

Taiyaki
NYC

Sunday In
Brooklyn

L'Industrie
Pizzeria

For All
Things Good

Leif

WILLIAMSBURG

This *Brooklyn* neighbourhood is known for its hipster vibe, *family-friendly atmosphere* and culture-rich activities. Offering up a great food scene, charming shops and sweeping views of the *Manhattan skyline,* Williamsburg is a great place to explore. Wandering through Williamsburg is a great *weekend activity,* with lots of great vintage and independent shops selling unique wares and European-style *bakeries* baking up fresh viennoiseries.

The Attic Brooklyn
231 Grand St, 11211
Well-organised vintage/thrift shop with a great atmosphere and assortment of clothes. Moseying through here is always a delight.

Bakeri
150 Wythe Ave, 11211
This rustic, Scandi-influenced bakery has a great selection of pastries and breads. It is a great place for breakfast or lunch and has delicious desserts as well.

Beam
272 Kent Ave, 11249
A bright home goods store with everything from small decorations to large furniture. You'll be sure to find inspiration for your home in this well-curated shop.

Catbird
108 N 7th St, 11249
This jewellery store is known for their forever bracelets, where a bracelet is welded to perfectly fit you. They also have a wonderful assortment of rings, necklaces and bracelets for every occasion, with lots of personalisation options.

Domino Park
15 River St, 11249
This riverside park has lovely views of Manhattan and is a great place to enjoy a picnic or a walk. There is also a fun kids' playground with views of the city.

Everlane
104 N 6th St, 11211
Known for their ethical approach to fashion and timeless designs, this clothing store is a great place to stock up on wardrobe staples.

For All Things Good
314 Grand St, 11211
You can taste the passion behind the food at this cosy Mexican eatery. Handmade tortillas are the star here, but everything is delicious.

Gelateria Gentile
253 Wythe Ave, 11249

Delicious gelato in a wonderful array of flavours. You can't go wrong with your flavour choice here.

Homecoming
92 Berry St, 11249

Come for the pastries and coffee, stay for the houseplants and flowers.

Leif
99 Grand St, 11249

This shop is filled with beautiful objects for your home, from kitchenware to stationery and artwork to candles.

L'Industrie Pizzeria
254 S 2nd St, 11211

Delicious pizzas, daily sandwich specials and lemon bombelone (an Italian doughnut) are all great reasons to go to this local favourite restaurant.

Nick + Sons Bakery
205 Leonard St, 11206

Some of the best croissants and pastries you'll find in New York. There is often a queue but it moves quickly.

Quimby's Bookstore
536 Metropolitan Ave, 11211

This indie bookshop has a finely curated stock of books as well as a wonderful assortment of zines.

Sunday In Brooklyn
348 Wythe Ave, 11249

Enjoy some of the most delicious pancakes for brunch, great sandwiches and grain bowls for lunch and a wonderful selection of small plates and mains for dinner.

Taiyaki NYC
294 Bedford Ave, 11249

Enjoy soft serve ice cream in a fluffy fish cone or a mochi doughnut.

Brooklyn
Bridge

Washington
Street

Time Out
Market

Cecconi's

L'Appartement
4F

Brooklyn
Bridge Park

Yours Truly,
Brooklyn

BOOKS ARE MAGIC

French Louie

Books are Magic

Measure Twice

Caputo's
Bake Shop

Woods Grove

Wanderlustre

BROOKLYN HEIGHTS

Brooklyn Heights is one of the *most charming* village-like places you can explore in New York. With quaint, tree-lined streets, elegant brownstones, bakeries, *independent shops*, restaurants and sweeping views of Manhattan, it is no wonder this area is *popular* with locals and visitors alike. Enjoy the views from Brooklyn Bridge Park, walk down Willow, Cranberry or Orange Streets and enjoy looking at the facades of the brownstones, or head to one of the *charming bakeries* for a freshly baked treat. After exploring the area, you can walk across Brooklyn Bridge or grab drinks with friends at the Time Out Market, both offering *unrivalled views* of lower Manhattan.

Books are Magic

122 Montague St, Brooklyn Heights, 11201

A well-curated bookstore with an amazing selection of books. The staff recommendations are great, and the children's section is charming.

Brooklyn Bridge

Prospect St and Washington St Intersection

A walk along the pedestrian path of Brooklyn Bridge is one of those must-do things in NYC. At just over a mile long, the path offers stunning views. It tends to be less crowded early in the day or later in the evening.

Brooklyn Bridge Park

334 Furman St, Brooklyn, 11201

This is one of the most scenic parks in New York. With views for days and fun places to stop, it is a great place to stroll through. At the north end of the park is Jane's Carousel, a hundred-year-old ride that has been lovingly restored. Further south along the park are piers which offer stunning lookouts. It is a great place to picnic with family or friends when the weather is good.

Caputo's Bake Shop

329 Court St, Cobble Hill, 11231

This old-school Italian bakery offers up delicious bread, cakes, pastries and cookies.

Cecconi's

55 Water St, Dumbo, 11201

If you are looking for a nice place for a leisurely meal, book a table here. With lovely views of Manhattan and the Brooklyn Bridge, as well as great Italian food, it will be a meal to remember.

French Louie

320 Atlantic Ave, Brooklyn, 11201

If you are going for lunch or dinner, the steak frites is delicious. For brunch get the crème brûlée French toast.

L'Appartement 4F

115 Montàgue St, Brooklyn Heights, 11201

Pastries, cookies and artisan bread are all on offer here. Get there earlier in the day if you want a flavoured croissant.

Measure Twice

225 Court St, Cobble Hill, 11201

Charming stationery and gift shop with a wide selection of unique products.

Time Out Market

55 Water St, Dumbo, 11201

For great food and exceptional views, Time Out Market is the place to go. There is a rooftop bar and terrace offering views of Brooklyn Bridge, as well as a great selection of food vendors.

Washington Street

Washington St, Dumbo, 11201

The view from this street of the Empire State Building nestled under Manhattan Bridge has made this street a popular photography spot for tourists.

Woods Grove

302 Court St, Cobble Hill, 11231

This unique gift shop offers a great mix of goods from local-made to vintage.

Yours Truly, Brooklyn

680 Fulton St, Brooklyn, 11217

A wonderful assortment of cards, stationery, pens and notebooks.

Wanderlustre

262 Court St, Cobble Hill, 11231

A fun selection of home goods and gifts. A great place to find something for a friend's birthday or a little something special for yourself.

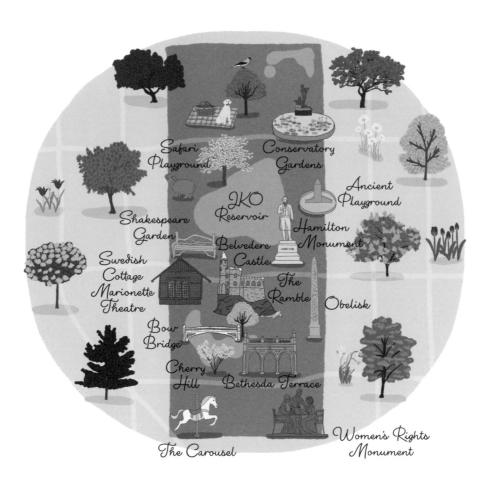

Safari Playground

Conservatory Gardens

Ancient Playground

JKO Reservoir

Hamilton Monument

Shakespeare Garden

Belvedere Castle

Swedish Cottage Marionette Theatre

The Ramble

Obelisk

Bow Bridge

Cherry Hill

Bethesda Terrace

The Carousel

Women's Rights Monument

CENTRAL PARK

NEW YORK BY LOCALS

Central Park is rightly popular with locals and tourists alike. And it's no wonder why, with its sweeping vantage points, running and cycling trails, plus dozens of children's playgrounds. In springtime the park *comes alive* as it fills with cherry blossoms and blooming flowers; in summer it is a great place to have a *picnic* or take a shaded walk in the Ramble. As the weather turns cooler you can see *vibrant leaves* on the abundant trees throughout the park, and in the winter it becomes a frosty oasis blanketed with snow. Wandering through the park is a true joy, and a *definite must* if you are visiting NYC.

Belvedere Castle
Mid-park at 79th St

Climb the castle's ramparts for sweeping views of Central Park. Be sure to check out Turtle Pond and see how many turtles you can spot.

Bethesda Terrace and Fountain
Mid-park at 72nd St

Bethesda Terrace's beautiful architecture and fountain make it a popular destination. Enjoy the views from the terrace or rent a boat and paddle around the Lake.

Bow Bridge
Mid-park at 73rd St

This beautiful Victorian bridge offers sweeping views of the Lake and is a great way to get from the Ramble to Bethesda Terrace.

The Carousel
Mid-park at 65th St

A popular place to stop off with kids, this charming carousel dating back to 1908 has been an enduring part of the park.

Cherry Hill
Mid-park at 72nd St

In springtime the cherry trees on this hill blossom, making it a wonderful spot for a spring picnic. With views of the Lake, you can watch boaters sweep past as you enjoy the scenery.

Conservatory Gardens
E 105th St, Upper East Side

Enter through the Vanderbilt Gate to explore the only formal garden in Central Park. Enjoy the daffodils and draping wisteria in early spring, and roses and lily pads in the summer.

Jacqueline Kennedy Onassis Reservoir
Mid-park between 86th and 96th St

A walk around this reservoir offers up stunning views year-round but especially in springtime when the pink cherry blossoms are in bloom.

Obelisk
E 81st St, Upper East Side
Located behind The Met, this Egyptian obelisk is around 3,500 years old. Gifted to the US by the Egyptian Government in the 1870s, it has been on display in Central Park for nearly 150 years.

Playgrounds
All over the park
There are 21 playgrounds dotted across Central Park. From Ancient Playground near The Met to the Safari Playground, there are playgrounds that have it all. Covering water to sand and climbing to toddler-friendly, there are so many options for places for kids to stop and play.

The Ramble
Mid-park between 73rd and 79th St
This densely packed woodland area is designed to make you feel like you are in a forest and not a huge city.

Shakespeare Garden
Mid-park, W 79th St, Upper West Side
This beautiful garden has been landscaped with flowers and plants that are mentioned in Shakespeare's sonnets and plays.

Swedish Cottage Marionette Theatre
Mid-park, W 79th St, Upper West Side
This charming cottage has lived many lives, but since the 1970s it has been a family-friendly marionette theatre, enchanting children of all ages with whimsical performances.

Monuments
Throughout the park
Dotted throughout are monuments celebrating everyone from suffragettes, who fought for women's rights, to Alexander Hamilton, a founding father.

Lighthouse
Park

Panorama
Room

The Noguchi
Museum

Magnolia
Bakery

Blackwell House

ROOSEVELT ISLAND

Roosevelt Island Tram

Smallpox
Memorial
Hospital

PEPSI COLA

City Viewpoint

Four Freedoms
State Park

ROOSEVELT ISLAND

This small island is *rich* with history and is a great place to explore, especially on a sunny day. If you are visiting from the Manhattan side, you should take the *Roosevelt Tram*, which is a quick ride across the East River. The island is about two miles in length and you can walk around it easily in a few hours. With *historic homes*, hospitals and a storied history, there are plenty of places to *explore* for a nice day out. There are also Citi Bikes on the island, so if you prefer *exploring* via bicycle that is a great option as well.

Blackwell House
500 Main St, Roosevelt Island, 10044
Built in 1796, this home is one of the oldest surviving farmhouses in NYC. It has been extensively refurbished and you can tour it Wednesday to Sunday to learn about the history of the island through the small exhibit they have.

City Viewpoint
Loop Rd, Roosevelt Island, 10044
This grassy knoll does what it says, offering up city views of both Brooklyn and Manhattan. A great place to wander through on your way to or from Four Freedoms State Park.

Four Freedoms State Park
Roosevelt Island, 10044
Located at the southern end of the island, this state park is truly stunning. With brutalist granite slabs framing stunning views and tree-lined walkways leading to the tip of the park, it is a wonderful place to explore.

Lighthouse Park
910 Main St, Roosevelt Island, 10044
At the northernmost end of the island is Lighthouse Park, which has a towering lighthouse built in 1872. A newer addition to the park is the beautiful memorial, The Girl Puzzle, honouring journalist and trailblazer Nellie Bly.

Magnolia Bakery
1000 3rd Ave, Upper East Side, 10022
If you are taking the Roosevelt Tram from Manhattan, I'd highly recommend stopping into the Magnolia Bakery located in Bloomingdale's on E 60th Street to pick up some desserts to enjoy while you are on the island.

The Noguchi Museum

9-01 33rd Rd, Queens, 11106

If you are near the Roosevelt Island Bridge,
it's worth popping over to Astoria to visit the
Noguchi Museum, which was designed and
built by the artist himself.

Panorama Room

22 North Loop Rd, Roosevelt Island, 10044

The rooftop bar of the Graduate Hotel offers up truly spectacular views.
If you time it right you can watch the sunset over the city.

Roosevelt Island Tram

254 E 60th St, Upper East Side, 10022

The five minute ride from the Upper East Side to Roosevelt Island
offers sweeping skyline views.

Smallpox Memorial Hospital

Roosevelt Island, 10044

The ruins of this hospital are spectacularly dramatic. With ivy growing
over the stone walls, this historic hospital has been stabilised so it doesn't
continue to crumble. This was the first purpose-built smallpox hospital in
the United States, and people who contracted smallpox were isolated to
quell the spread.

NEW YORK

BY INTEREST

PART THREE

BOOKSTORES + CHARMING STREETS + MUSEUMS + BEST VIEWS
+ CYCLING NYC + LITERARY NYC + NYC WITH KIDS + REVOLUTIONARY NYC
+ SPEAKEASIES + STREET ART

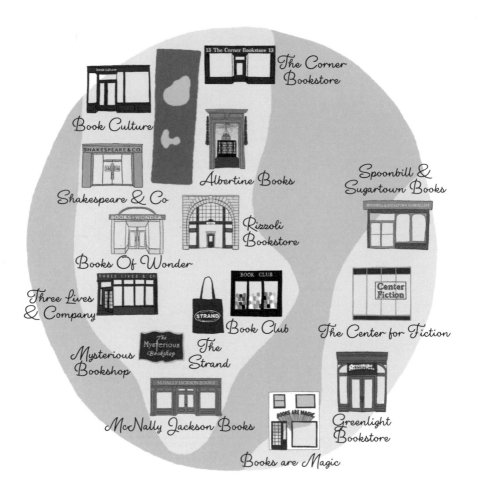

The Corner Bookstore

Book Culture

Albertine Books

Spoonbill & Sugartown Books

Shakespeare & Co

Rizzoli Bookstore

Books Of Wonder

Three Lives & Company

Book Club

The Center for Fiction

The Strand

Mysterious Bookshop

McNally Jackson Books

Greenlight Bookstore

Books are Magic

BOOKSTORES

Exploring bookstores is one of the best ways to discover a city: each individual bookshop reflects its surrounding neighbourhood. Bookstores are truly my *happy place* and I make a point of visiting them no matter what city I am in. There is nothing I love more than perusing the tables of staff recommendations, seeing what local authors have written and *exploring* the children's book section to find books my daughter might be interested in. Plus, New York has a *deep literary* history and the dozens of bookstores dotted across the city reflect this.

Albertine Books

972 5th Ave, Upper East Side, 10075

A stunning bookstore offering up a great selection of French and English books. Wandering through here will transport you straight to Paris.

Book Club

197 E 3rd St, East Village, 10009

A cosy bookshop offering up coffee during the day and drinks at night, with a busy calendar of rotating events.

Book Culture

Two locations in Morningside Heights

An extensive selection of new and used books and textbooks located near the Columbia campus.

Books are Magic

Multiple locations, Cobble Hill, Brooklyn Heights

Wonderfully curated and bright selection of books. Lots of great staff recommendations and literary events for adults and children.

Books Of Wonder

42 W 17th St, Chelsea, 10011

A delightful children's bookshop with a great selection of new and rare children's books. They also have a great kid's story time for young ones.

The Center for Fiction

15 Lafayette Ave, Brooklyn, 11217

A beautiful bookstore with frequent events and workshops as well as a great café where you can read your latest acquisitions.

The Corner Bookstore

1313 Madison Ave, Upper East Side, 10128

A charming, quaint bookshop that has a wonderful atmosphere and a fine selection of books.

Greenlight Bookstore

Multiple locations, Fort Greene, Flatbush

On top of selling a wonderful selection of books, Greenlight boasts several book clubs, children's story time, and an array of literary events.

McNally Jackson Books

Multiple locations, Downtown Brooklyn, Seaport, Williamsburg, Nolita

A cosy bookshop with an extensive selection of books; a true gem for bibliophiles to explore.

Mysterious Bookshop

58 Warren St, Tribeca, 10007

With books from the floor to ceiling, this is the place to go if you are on the lookout for crime, detective or mystery books.

Rizzoli Bookstore

1133 Broadway, Flatiron, 10010

A literary oasis for browsing unique art, architecture and design books, as well as a beautifully curated section of kids, popular and local books.

Shakespeare & Co

Multiple locations, Upper East Side, Upper West Side

A delightful bookstore, with a coffee shop as well as a diverse selection of books.

Spoonbill and Sugartown Books

218 Bedford Ave, Brooklyn, 11211

This book shop is a local favourite. You'll be sure to finds something unique while browsing the shelves

The Strand

Multiple locations, Union Square, Upper West Side

A NY institution since the 1920s, this bookstore is a must-visit for any book lover. You are sure to find something that catches your eye.

Three Lives & Company

154 W 10th St, Greenwich, 10014

This bookstore might be small but it is extremely well-curated. From local authors to bestsellers, the selection is great.

Greenwich
Village

Washington
Mews

Stuyvesant
Street

Central Park
West

Pomander
Walk

Washington
Street

Brooklyn
Heights

Murray
Hill

Upper East Side

Cobble Hill

Kent Street

Gramercy Park

CHARMING STREETS

NEW YORK BY INTEREST

Dotted amongst the high-rises and *giant apartment* blocks of New York are charming streets that feel like you are a world away from the *hustle and bustle* of the city. From idyllic brownstones to tree-lined streets, ivy-covered houses to sleepy mews streets that look as though they were plucked from a *bygone-era* New York, there is quaintness and charm to be found in every corner of the city. Wandering through Brooklyn Heights will make you dream of moving to New York; a stroll through The Village will show off the *quaint streets* filled with great cafes and shops; and Washington Mews will transport you to old-time New York, when the streets were cobbled and *horse-drawn carriages* were the preferred mode of transportation.

Brooklyn Heights

Brooklyn, 11201

The historic neighbourhood of Brooklyn Heights is full of charming brownstones, most built in the mid 1800s. Be sure to stroll down Cranberry Street, Willow Street, Pineapple Street, Columbia Heights, Grace Court Alley, Joralemon Street and Hunts Lane.

Central Park West

Central Park and 85th St

The majority the homes originally built on Central Park West have over time been converted into huge apartment complexes, but there are few holdouts and it's interesting to see the juxtaposition of old-world New York against the relatively newer buildings.

Cobble Hill

Brooklyn, 11201

An enchanting area with red-brick homes and tree-lined streets. The entire area is fun to wander through – don't miss Warren Place and Baltic Street, and look through the gate of Warren Place Mews.

Gramercy Park

Gramercy, 10003

Irving Place, Gramercy Park West and Rutherford Place are beautiful streets full of homes with lots of character. From the gas lampposts still burning in front of Gramercy Park West houses to the ivy-covered facades of Irving Place, this is a gorgeous area to explore.

Greenwich Village

Greenwich Village, 10014

Greenwich Village has no shortage of charm. When wandering around, don't miss Gay Street, Minetta Street, West 10th (between 5th and 6th), West 9th Street, Waverly Place or MacDougal Street.

Kent Street

Greenpoint, Brooklyn, 11222

This charming Greenpoint street is lined with idyllic brownstones. There are lots of great shops and cafes in the neighbourhood as well – pop into Archestratus Books + Foods or Old Fox Coffee.

Murray Hill

Murray Hill, 10016

East 38th Street is home to some beautiful townhouses; wander a few blocks down and you will find the charming Sniffen Court.

Pomander Walk

Upper West Side, 10025

Enjoy the Tudor-inspired facades along 94th and peak into Pomander Walk, a private street with charming houses that you would not expect to find in the middle of a city.

Stuyvesant Street

East Village, 10003

This East Village Street is home to another iconic NYC building, the Renwick Triangle, that loves to be photographed. With dramatic foliage and interesting architecture, it is no wonder why. Pair it with a visit to Ruby's Cafe for a delicious Aussie-style brunch.

Upper East Side

Old and new buildings collide on the Upper East Side, and there are lots of charming streets to explore. Don't miss East 69th Street, East 65th East 70th, East 71st and East 78th Streets between park and Lexington, as well as East 80th Street between Lexington and 3rd Ave.

Washington Mews

Greenwich Village, 10003

A charming cobbled mews located just north of Washington Square Park. As New York has grown and changed, this street has maintained its sense of charm and quaintness.

Washington Street

Dumbo, Brooklyn, 11201

If you are wanting THAT picture with the Manhattan Bridge, Empire State Building and a cobbled street, this is the place to go. This street is super popular for taking photos so be prepared.

Cooper Hewitt, Smithsonian
Design Museum

The Guggenheim

The Met Cloisters

Neue Galerie

American Museum
of Natural History

The Met

The Noguchi
Museum

The Frick
Collection

Whitney
Museum of
American Art

The
MOMA

Merchant's House
Museum

Ellis Island National
Museum of Immigration

MUSEUMS

Museums are such *wonderful places*: we can experience history, stories, learn something new or see things from a different perspective, as well as so much more. New York has some of the best *museums* in the world, with world-class collections ranging from *prehistoric fossils* to contemporary art. Most of these museums are extensive in both content and scale, and you won't be able to see everything, but the *variety of museums* available in New York means you'll be able to find something that interests you. If you are into Contemporary American Art, be sure to visit the Whitney; if European Masters are your favourite, then a visit to the Frick is a must. For a nice day out, the Met Cloisters is lovely, and if you like a museum with a delicious cafe then the Neue Galerie is the place to go.

American Museum of Natural History
200 Central Park West, Upper West Side, 10024
From star shows in the planetarium to the Hall of Saurischian Dinosaurs, there are endless things to discover and learn about at this iconic museum.

Cooper Hewitt, Smithsonian Design Museum
2 E 91st St, Upper East Side, 10128
Housed within Carnegie Mansion, the Cooper Hewitt museum showcases design from around the world from ancient to modern times. The gardens are also stunning, so leave time to explore them before you go.

Ellis Island National Museum of Immigration
Ellis Island Bridge, Jersey City, NJ, 10280
The original migration offices that countless people have passed through. Discover their stories, names and what people left, sacrificed and endured to become an immigrant in America.

The Frick Collection
1 E 70th St, Upper East Side, 10021
Artwork from the European Masters is on display in this former residence turned museum. Enjoy paintings by Holbein, Van Dyck, Manet, Greco, Renoir, Velazquez, Rembrandt, Turner and more.

The Guggenheim
1071 5th Ave, Upper East Side, 10128
The building, designed by Frank Lloyd Wright, is designed as a giant spiral, allowing you to enjoy the museum's collection as you slowly meander your way down.

Merchant's House Museum
29 E 4th St, NoHo, 10003
A 19th-century home turned museum shows how life would have been for the Treadwell family and their servants and staff. All furniture, art and personal effects are original to the home.

The Met

1000 5th Ave, Upper East Side, 10028

Wandering through The Met is a delight. Be sure not to miss the
immaculate Temple of Dendur, an entire Frank Lloyd Wright room,
and the wonderful selection of art from European Masters to modern
classics. In the spring and summer head up to the rooftop bar to enjoy
the beautiful view of Central Park.

The Met Cloisters

99 Margaret Corbin Dr, Washington Heights, 10040

A wonderful collection of medieval artworks housed in a French
monastery with beautiful gardens and views of the Hudson. A truly
wonderful place to wander and explore.

The MOMA

11 W 53rd St, Midtown, 10019

This world-class museum features artwork from the most notable
modern artists. From Pollock to Warhol and Dali to Monet, this
museum covers everything from Impressionism to Surrealism.

Neue Galerie

1048 5th Ave, Upper East Side, 10028

Features prominent German and Austrian artwork from the early
20th century. Be sure to stop into Cafe Sabarsky for delicious
German desserts served in a cosy setting.

The Noguchi Museum

9-01 33rd Rd, Queens, 11106

A small but beautifully curated museum designed by Noguchi himself
and featuring a collection of his sculptures and work. His use of scale and
minimalistic design are as inspiring today as when he first created them.

Whitney Museum of American Art

99 Gansevoort St, Chelsea, 10014

This museum boasts an impressive collection of contemporary American
artwork accompanied by beautiful views over the Hudson.

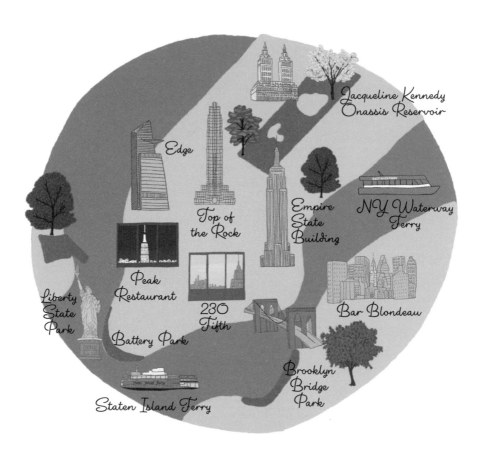

Jacqueline Kennedy Onassis Reservoir

Edge

Top of the Rock

Empire State Building

NY Waterway Ferry

Peak Restaurant

230 Fifth

Liberty State Park

Battery Park

Bar Blondeau

Brooklyn Bridge Park

Staten Island Ferry

BEST VIEWS

New York is a city that loves to be looked at, and there are so many *amazing viewpoints* from which to enjoy the *spectacular* skyline. There are your traditional observation decks offering up *sweeping views* from the city's highest buildings, parks, ferries and water taxis, as well as *walking paths* that offer up striking backdrops of the *skyscrapers* and buildings that make up this concrete jungle.

VIEW FROM THE TOP

If you enjoy seeing things from up high then don't miss out on these great observation decks.

Edge
30 Hudson Yards, Chelsea, 10001
An observation deck 100 stories high with a glass floor.

Empire State Building
20 W 34th St, Midtown, 10001
Sweeping views of Manhattan from the top of an iconic skyscraper.

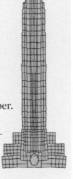

Top of the Rock
30 Rockefeller Plaza, Midtown, 10112
Stunning views of Manhattan.

MEALS WITH A VIEW

For a memorable meal with spectacular views try out one of these.

230 Fifth
230 5th Ave, 10001
Rooftop bar with sweeping city views. Great place to grab drink.

Bar Blondeau
80 Wythe Ave 6th Floor, Brooklyn, 11249
This Brooklyn bar has expansive views on the city.

Peak Restaurant
30 Hudson Yards 101st floor, 10001
Panoramic views of the city.

Robert
2 Columbus Cir, 10019
Views of Columbus Circle and Central Park serving food just as good as the views.

VIEWS FROM THE GROUND

There are amazing views to be had throughout the city, and sometimes all you need to do is look up.

Battery Park

Financial District, 10004

It's lovely to walk along the Esplanade, and there is a nice Statue of Liberty viewpoint as well.

Brooklyn Bridge Park

Brooklyn, 11201

Stunning views of Brooklyn Bridge and Manhattan.

Jacqueline Kennedy Onassis Reservoir

Central Park, Manhattan, 10128

A walk around this reservoir offers up beautiful views of the stunning buildings dotted around Central Park.

Liberty State Park

200 Morris Pesin Dr, Jersey City, NJ, 07305

This New Jersey park has stunning views of Manhattan and a beautiful 9/11 memorial.

NY Waterway Ferry

East River, from 90th St to Wall St

The NY Waterway ferry goes down along the East River offering stunning views of both Manhattan and Brooklyn. To enjoy all the views take it from 90th down to Wall Street.

Staten Island Ferry

4 South St, Financial District, 10004

A ride on the Staten Island Ferry offers up wonderful views of Lower Manhattan and the Statue of Liberty.

Central Park Loop

Hudson River Greenway

Roosevelt Island

Governors Island

Brooklyn Bridge Park to Red Hook

CYCLING NYC

One of the best ways to experience a big city is on a bike and New York has some great *dedicated* cycle paths offering up scenic views. With miles of paths to choose from, you can easily enjoy a long solo ride, a short ride with friends or make an entire day out of it. From enjoying a *quiet ride* through a park to trails offering up skyline views, these cycle paths provide a *fun and unique* way to explore the city. You can easily rent a Citi Bike from stations across the city, or if you are *biking* with younger ones opt for one of the many bike rental shops, especially near Central Park.

Central Park Loop

Cycling the Central Park loop is a wonderful place to escape the hustle and bustle of busy New York City. The cycle path here is mostly car free, making it an easy place to enjoy the outdoors.

Governors Island

Offering scenic views of Manhattan, Brooklyn and the Statue of Liberty, Governors Island is a wonderful place to take a leisurely cycle. This car-free island offers up tree-lined-trails and lots of history. Having been used as a military base off and on since before the Revolutionary War, the island now offers abundant green space, monuments and historical landmarks.

Hudson River Greenway

This cycle path runs the length of Manhattan, offering up scenic views of the Hudson River and landmarks along the way. From Battery Park at the southernmost tip to the Met Cloisters at the northern, this 13-mile path takes you past the World Trade Centre, the Intrepid Sea, Air, and Space Museum, Riverside Park, The Little Red Lighthouse and the Met Cloisters.

Roosevelt Island

This tranquil island has been used for many different purposes over the centuries and you can enjoy the history while cycling around the island. The easiest way to get to Roosevelt Island from Manhattan is the tram, which you can take your bike on. Be sure not to miss the Smallpox Memorial Hospital, the FDR Four Freedoms Park at the southern tip and Lighthouse Park at the north end.

Brooklyn Bridge Park to Red Hook

This short cycle path is a lovely waterfront route and has stunning views of Manhattan. Start at John Street Park, which is nestled next to Manhattan Bridge. Sticking to the park paths, you can wind your way around the waterfront past Brooklyn Bridge Park and down around to Red Hook. Be sure to stop at Valentino Pier for a great view of the Statue of Liberty. There are lots of restaurants, cafes and shops along the way, from the Time Out Market in Dumbo to Steve's Authentic Key Lime Pie and United Sandwiches of America in Red Hook.

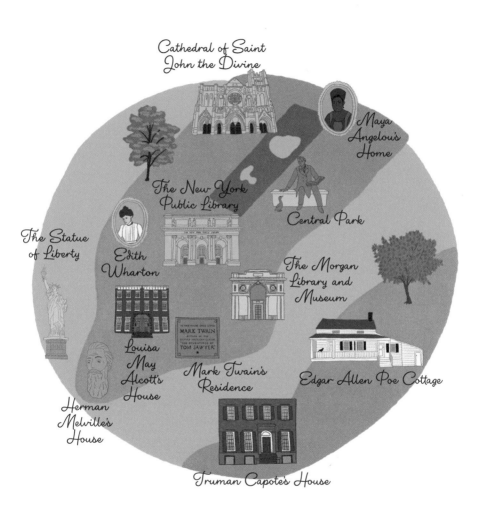

Cathedral of Saint John the Divine

Maya Angelou's Home

The New York Public Library

Central Park

The Statue of Liberty

Edith Wharton

The Morgan Library and Museum

Louisa May Alcott's House

Mark Twain's Residence

Edgar Allen Poe Cottage

Herman Melville's House

Truman Capote's House

LITERARY NYC

The city of New York has been influencing writers since its origins in the *seventeenth century* and has shaped some of the most famous American writers and poets. It is where aspiring writers go and popular writers flourish. From Alexander Hamilton writing about *independence* to the poetry of Edgar Allen Poe, this city has *nourished* some of the most esteemed authors. Although the city has grown and changed over time, its *influence* over writers has stayed; it is a testament to how the places we live *influence* who we are.

Cathedral of Saint John the Divine

1047 Amsterdam Ave, Morningside Heights, 10025

Home to the American Poet's Corner, a memorial to the great American poets such as Dickinson, Thoreau, Wharton and Frost.

Central Park

Mid-park from 66th to 72nd Streets

This large park is home to several statues celebrating literary icons such as Lewis Carroll's Alice, Mother Goose, Hans Christian Anderson, Shakespeare, Sir Walter Scott and Robert Burns.

Edgar Allen Poe Cottage

2640 Grand Concourse, The Bronx, 10458

This cottage is where Poe spent the last years of his life. It was due to be demolished in the 1900s but Poe's popularity led to public outcry and the home was preserved and turned into a museum.

Edith Wharton

14 W 23rd St, Flatiron, 10010

The ground floor Wharton's childhood home is now a Starbucks. Edith wrote about life in the Gilded Age and 1921 she became the first woman to win the Pulitzer Prize in Literature.

Herman Melville's House

6 Pearl St, 10004

Known most widely for writing the classic *Moby Dick*, Melville was born on Pearl Street in 1819. The house is no longer there but there is a plaque.

Louisa May Alcott's House

130 MacDougal St, Greenwich, 10012

The beloved book *Little Women* was finished here, where Ms Alcott was staying with her uncle and his family; it now belongs to NYU's Law School.

Mark Twain's Residence

14 West 10th St, Greenwich Village, 10011

Although now privately owned, Twain lived at this notoriously haunted building for about a year – and it's rumoured that his ghost is one of many who can be spotted there.

Maya Angelou's Home

58 W 120th St, Harlem, 10027

Renowned poet and writer Maya Angelou lived in New York on and off throughout her life. Her works *I Know Why The Caged Bird Sings* and *Still I Rise* are as relevant today as when they were written decades ago.

The Morgan Library and Museum

225 Madison Ave, Midtown, 10016

Like walking into a fairy tale, the Morgan features a gorgeous library with an extensive array of rare books.

The New York Public Library

Stephen A. Schwarzman Building 476 5th Ave, Midtown, 10018

Explore the library's treasures and alluring reading rooms, as well as beautiful murals and paintings.

The Statue of Liberty

Liberty Island, 10004

The base of The Statue of Liberty has the poem "The New Colossus" by Emma Lazarus inscribed, with the famous line "Give me your tired, your poor, your huddled masses yearning to breathe free . . ."

Truman Capote's House

70 Willow St, Brooklyn Heights, 11201

Capote lived in this Brooklyn home for 10 years, during which time he completed *In Cold Blood*, *Breakfast at Tiffany's* and *Brooklyn Heights: A Personal Memoir*. It is now privately owned.

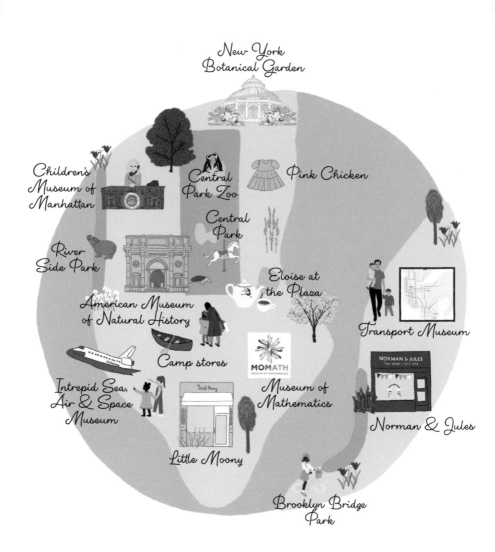

New York
Botanical Garden

Children's
Museum of
Manhattan

Central
Park Zoo

Pink Chicken

Central
Park

River
Side Park

Eloise at
the Plaza

American Museum
of Natural History

Transport Museum

Camp stores

MOMATH
MUSEUM OF MATHEMATICS

Museum of
Mathematics

Intrepid Sea,
Air & Space
Museum

NORMAN & JULES
TOY SHOP — EST. 2013

Norman & Jules

Little Moony

Brooklyn Bridge
Park

NYC WITH KIDS

New York is a great place to explore with kids of all ages. There are so many *wonderful* museums, playgrounds, parks, theatres and shops that leave you spoilt for choice when it comes to deciding on what to do. My biggest piece of advice when travelling with kids, especially in a big city, is not to *overdo* it. Pick one or two activities the kids will enjoy and *intersperse* that with your own preferences. And, if all else fails, I find a visit to a playground or a park is always a good plan.

On multiple occasions I have spent an entire morning or afternoon in a *playground* while on holiday and have met some lovely locals, who often have *great suggestions* for places to eat and explore.

New York Botanical Garden

2900 Southern Blvd, The Bronx, 10458

Sprawling gardens that are a joy to explore year-round.
The perfect place to let young ones experience nature.

Brooklyn Bridge Park

Brooklyn Heights, 11201

Fun playgrounds, water features and stunning views makes
this park enjoyable for the whole family.

CAMP stores

Multiple locations, Chelsea, Union Square, Brooklyn

This toy store is so much more than just a store; there is an array
of activities and areas for kids to play in and explore.

Central Park

Manhattan

With 21 playgrounds to choose from, Central Park is a great place to take
kids of all ages. There is also a carousel, Swedish Cottage Marionette
Theatre, The Belvedere Castle and the Turtle Pond.

Central Park Zoo

East 64th St, Central Park, Manhattan, 10021

This small zoo packs in a lot of animals. Don't miss the penguins
or red pandas!

Children's Museum of Manhattan

212 W 83rd St, Upper West Side, 10024

Geared more towards younger children, this interactive museum has lots
of wonderful spaces and fun activities for imaginative and creative play.

Eloise at the Plaza

1 W 58th St, Central Park South, 10019

Visit The Plaza Hotel for a charming Eloise-Themed children's afternoon
tea and the delightful Eloise gift shop.

Intrepid Sea, Air & Space Museum
Pier 86, 12th Ave & W 46th St, Hell's Kitchen, 10036
Explore the inside of an aircraft carrier, see the close quarters on
a submarine and be amazed at the size of the space shuttle.

Little Moony
230 Mulberry St, Nolita, 10012
A children's shop with a beautiful curation of toys, games and clothing.

National Museum of Mathematics
11 E 26th St, Flatiron, 10010
A fun interactive museum with engaging and unique ways to learn
about mathematics. The staff are amazing as well.

American Museum of Natural History
200 Central Park West, Upper West Side, 10024
From star shows in the planetarium to prehistoric dinosaur fossils,
this museum is rightly a favourite for kids of all ages.

Norman & Jules
68 3rd St, Brooklyn, 11231
A beautiful selection of children's toys and clothes that you would
be proud to keep on permanent display.

Pink Chicken
Multiple locations, Upper East Side, West Village
Cheerful clothing for kids and women featuring fun prints in classic styles.

River Side Park
Upper West Side
Featuring 13 playgrounds, Riverside Park is also a great place to
take kids. The themed playgrounds are especially well done.

Transport Museum
99 Schermerhorn St, Brooklyn, 11201
Housed in an old Subway station, this museum has wonderful
exhibits about the history of the city.

Morris-Jumel
Mansion

Van Cortlandt
House Museum

New-York
Historical Society

Hamilton Grange

City Hall
Park

Trinity
Church

Federal Hall

Bowling
Green

The Conference House

Fraunces
Tavern

The Old Stone House

REVOLUTIONARY NYC

Native Americans had been living in New York for centuries before the Dutch came in 1624. It wasn't until 1665 that the British took control and changed the name to *New York*. After one hundred years of British rule, the people living in New York were no longer happy being part of the British Empire. Revolutionaries claimed taxation without representation was unjust and that their interests had *diverged* from that of Britain. This spurred the Revolutionary War, which was fought between 1775 and 1783, with America ultimately winning. Several of these battles were fought in present-day New York City, including the *Battle of Brooklyn*, the Battle of Harlem Heights and the Battle of Fort Washington. Although New York would have been unrecognisable to what it has since become, there are still a handful of places that have stood steadfast and retain their revolutionary history.

Bowling Green
Broadway & Whitehall St, Financial District, 10004
This small park is the oldest in New York City. In 1776 revolutionaries pulled down a statue of King George III, which was then melted down and turned into bullets for the soldiers.

City Hall Park
Broadway & Chambers, St Tribeca, 10007
Five days after the Declaration of Independence was signed, George Washington read it to his Continental Army troops at this park.

The Conference House
7455 Hylan Blvd, Staten Island, 10307
It was on this site that unsuccessful peace talks were held between the British (represented by Commander-in-Chief William Howe) and the Americans (represented by Benjamin Franklin and John Adams).

Federal Hall
26 Wall St, Financial District, 10005
New York was the first capitol of the United States of America. It was on this site where George Washington became the first president and the First Congress was held.

Fraunces Tavern
54 Pearl St, Financial District, 10004
One of New York's oldest buildings, built in 1719, Fraunces was a favourite watering hole for America's founding fathers. George Washington used this building as his headquarters during the Revolutionary War. Today it is a museum and restaurant.

Hamilton Grange National Memorial
414 W 141st St, Harlem, 10031
Enjoy a guided tour through Alexander Hamilton's uptown home. Having been intended for demolition several times, it was granted the distinction of historical landmark and has been fully restored.

Morris-Jumel Mansion

65 Jumel Terrace, Washington Heights, 10032

Manhattan's oldest surviving home has hosted some of the most prominent founding fathers, including George Washington who used it as his base during the Battle of Harlem Heights in 1776.

New-York Historical Society

170 Central Park West, Upper West Side, 10024

New York's City's oldest museum covers 400 years of history, including an expansive collection with a focus on the Revolutionary War.

The Old Stone House

336 3rd St, Park Slope, 11215

It was on this site that in 1776 the Battle of Brooklyn took place. You can tour the house, learn about the battle and discover what colonial life was like.

Van Cortlandt House Museum

6036 Broadway, Van Cortlandt Park, The Bronx, 10471

Built in 1749, this was used a handful of times by George Washington during the Revolutionary War. The Van Cortlandt family had a plantation here as well which held enslaved Africans from the late 1600s until 1823.

Trinity Church

89 Broadway, Financial District, 10006

Erected at the end of the 17th century, three churches have stood on this ground, the last built in 1846. The churchyard houses the graves of many prominent figures in the American Revolution, including Alexander Hamilton.

UES

Please
Don't Tell

Bathtub Gin

Patent
Pending

The Hidden Pearl

PS at Pine & Polk

The Back
Room

SPEAKEASIES

The prohibition of the 1920s led to the rise of speakeasies. These *secret bars* were hidden behind restaurants, cafes and shops and the drinks were made with homemade alcohol, often *brewed* right on site. Often quite small, and cleverly hidden, these were places where people could go to *enjoy* an evening out. While prohibition only lasted a dozen years, the spirit of New York's *speakeasies* lives on. Step back in time with these lovely speakeasies and experience a bit of New York history without the threat of *breaking the law*. Book in advance if you can – wait times to get in can be quite long.

The Back Room

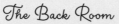

102 Norfolk St, Lower East Side, 10002
One of NYC's original speakeasies, where
you can enjoy your drink in a teacup
while listening to the bands play.

Bathtub Gin

132 9th Ave, Chelsea, 10011
This prohibition-era speakeasy will make you feel like you are in
1920s' NYC. Enter through Stone Street Coffee to enjoy this great
place, which also has live jazz and burlesque throughout the week.

The Hidden Pearl

621 Manhattan Ave, Greenpoint, Brooklyn, 11222
This cocktail bar is in the back of Wanpaku, a Japanese ramen
restaurant. It has a great selection of small plates and drinks,
all served up in a dark and quaint atmosphere.

Patent Pending

49 W 27th St, Flatiron, 10001
Enter through Patent Coffee to find this cosy cocktail bar with
drinks inspired by Nicola Tesla, the famous inventor, who lived
and worked in this building.

Please Don't Tell

113 St Marks Pl, East Village, 10009

Find the secret door in the phone booth and dial 1 to get from Crif Dogs into Please Don't Tell. A truly fun experience and you can enjoy a hot dog while you wait, or one on your way out.

PS at Pine & Polk

300 Spring St, Soho, 10013

This modern speakeasy is behind a hidden wall in Pine & Polk, an upscale supermarket selling a wonderful array of goods. They have a great selection of drinks and nibbles and the ambiance is cosy.

UES

1707 2nd Ave, Upper East Side, 10128

This pink ice cream shop doubles as a speakeasy. With creativedrinks, this unique speakeasy also has "Cinema Sundays", where you can enjoy a drink and a movie.

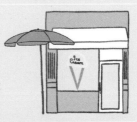

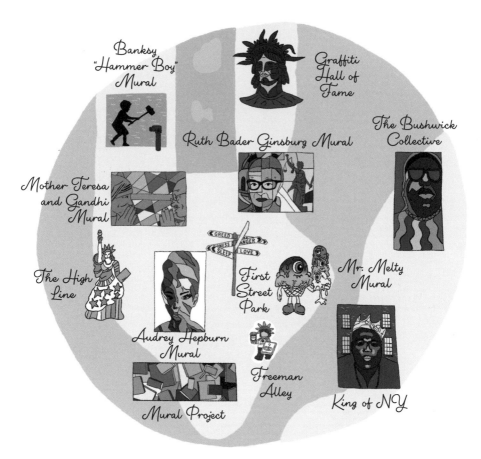

Banksy "Hammer Boy" Mural

Graffiti Hall of Fame

Ruth Bader Ginsburg Mural

The Bushwick Collective

Mother Teresa and Gandhi Mural

The High Line

First Street Park

Mr. Melty Mural

Audrey Hepburn Mural

Freeman Alley

Mural Project

King of NY

STREET ART

Since the 1970s street art has been a staple of New York City's *endless walls*, subway platforms and rolling shop grills. Once seen as a nuisance, this form of art is now *celebrated* and preserved across the city. The evolution of street art over the decades has led to it becoming a truly *stunning* form of art, with world-renowned artists creating *masterpieces* all over New York.

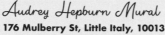

Audrey Hepburn Mural
176 Mulberry St, Little Italy, 10013
This beautiful mural in Little Italy is vibrant and worth stopping to admire. Pop into Cafe Roma to enjoy a cannoli while you admire the view.

Banksy "Hammer Boy" Mural
233 W 79th St, Upper West Side, 10024
This 2013 Banksy mural has been preserved thanks to a plexiglass covering and is currently the only public Banksy in New York.

The Bushwick Collective
427 Troutman St, Bushwick, Brooklyn, 11237
An eclectic collection of murals and graffiti running down an entire street. From the abstract to the surreal and everything in-between, it is a great place to see some unique street art.

Freeman Alley
Lower East Side, 10002
This alleyway is full of an eclectic array of graffiti and small murals.

Graffiti Hall of Fame
E 106th Street and Park Ave, Upper East Side, 10029
A school wall is the canvas for well known street artists showing off their talents and skill.

The High Line
Chelsea, 10011
The High Line has several sculptures, murals and art installations that you can enjoy while you walk down its plant-lined path.

King of NY

169 Quincy St, Brooklyn, 11216

Celebrating the Brooklyn native the Notorious B.I.G. (aka Biggie), who grew up in this neighbourhood, this multi-storey tribute is a must-visit for any fan.

Mother Teresa and Gandhi Mural

516-500 W 18th St, Chelsea, 10011

Vibrant colours and abstract shapes work in harmony to create this wonderful tribute to two historical icons of peace, unity and love.

Mr. Melty Mural

Chrystie St & Broome St, Lower East Side, 10002

This playful melty monster mural brightens up this Lower East Side street corner.

Mural Project

Two World Trade Center, Financial District, 10007

Vibrant murals cover the walls across from the World Trade Center, contrasting with the grey and silver skyscrapers surrounding this area.

Ruth Bader Ginsburg Mural

177 1st Ave, East Village, 10003

This expansive and colourful mural celebrates RBG, who was a New York native.

First Street Green Cultural Park

33 E 1st St, Lower East Side, 10003

This small park is full of amazing street art that is ever changing.

NEW YORK

BY SEASON

PART FOUR

The Met Cloisters

New York Botanical Garden

Picnic in Central Park

Walk the High Line

See a Show

Chelsea Art Galleries

Eataly Cooking Class

Gantry Plaza State Park

Sunset Sail

Village Vanguard

Nitehawk Cinema

ROMANTIC NYC

There are *endless* ways to spend quality time with your favourite people, especially in the 'city that never sleeps'. And there is no 'right' way to be romantic. We can show *our love* for others in many different ways – it might be a *kind* word, a gift or a hug. These ideas are *perfect* to enjoy with anyone you love, be it your *sweetheart*, best friend, furry friend or family.

New York Botanical Garden

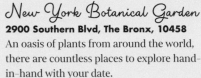

2900 Southern Blvd, The Bronx, 10458
An oasis of plants from around the world,
there are countless places to explore hand–
in-hand with your date.

Chelsea Art Galleries

Chelsea
On Thursday evenings the neighbourhood livens up with dozens
of galleries staying open late for Gallery Night, a unique and fun
way to see a lot of art while sipping on a nice drink.

Eataly Cooking Class

Multiple locations, Flatiron, Downtown
Enjoy making pasta, pizza and mozzarella or tasting cheese
and wine in one of the many classes Eataly offers.

Gantry Plaza State Park

Long Island City, 11101
Beautiful Midtown views with ample walkways and
benches to view them from.

The Met Cloisters

99 Margaret Corbin Dr, Washington Heights, 10040
Walking through the rebuilt medieval cloisters and monastery
while taking in the wonderful collection is lovely.

Nitehawk Cinema

Multiple locations, Prospect Park, Williamsburg
Enjoy drinks and nibbles while you watch a film. From new releases
to classics, an evening at the Nitehawk is sure to be fun.

Picnic in Central Park
Manhattan

Conservatory Gardens, Strawberry Fields and Pilgrim Hill are all lovely places to sit down for a picnic with your favourite someone.

See a Show
Broadway, 1006

New York has one of the best theatre scenes in the world. From world-class plays and musicals to the opera and ballet, it's a fabulous way to spend an evening out.

Sunset Sail Pier
Pier62, Chelsea Piers, Chelsea, 10011

Enjoy a picturesque sail in a schooner, taking in the sparkling lights of the city as the sun sets. A beautiful way to spend the evening.

Village Vanguard
178 7th Ave S, West Village, 10014

A cosy atmosphere and top-notch jazz bands are a perfect pairing for a date here.

Walk the High Line
Chelsea, 10011

An easy date night, with great views and lots of options for places to stop and eat or drink.

New York
Botanical Garden

Central
Park

Roosevelt
Island

Riverside
Park

The Frick
Collection

Brooklyn
Botanic Garden

Bryant Park

Maddison
Square
Park

Union
Square Park

Prospect Park

Washington
Square Park

Grace
Church

Green-Wood
Cemetery

NYC IN SPRING

There is something about seeing spring *blossoms*
against the backdrop of skyscrapers, historic
buildings and *iconic* landmarks that makes
springtime *extra special.* As the marks of winter
slowly fade and the days become longer, NYC
blossoms, its parks filling with *colour*
and signs of new life.

The Frick Collection
1 E 70th St, Upper East Side, 10021
Magnolias.

New York Botanical Garden
2900 Southern Blvd, The Bronx, 10458
Cherry blossoms, daffodils, tulips, roses.

Brooklyn Botanic Garden
990 Washington Ave, Brooklyn, 11225
Cherry blossoms, daffodils, tulips, roses.

Bryant Park
Midtown, 10018
Daffodils, tulips.

Central Park
Manhattan
Cherry blossoms, daffodils, tulips, roses, wisteria, magnolias.

Grace Church
802 Broadway, East Village, 10003
Magnolias.

Green-Wood Cemetery
500 25th St, Brooklyn, 11232
Cherry blossoms.

Maddison Square Park
11 Madison Ave, 10010
Cherry blossoms.

Prospect Park
Brooklyn, 11215
Cherry blossoms.

Riverside Park
From 72nd to 158th St along the Hudson River
Cherry blossoms, magnolias, daffodils, tulips.

Roosevelt Island
East River
Cherry blossoms.

Union Square Park
W &, E 17th St, Union Square, 10003
Cherry blossoms.

Washington Square Park
Washington Sq, Greenwich Village, 10012
Cherry blossoms, magnolias.

Spring Blossom to Watch for:

FEBRUARY to MARCH: Daffodils

APRIL: Magnolias

APRIL to MAY: Cherry blossoms, tulips, wisteria

JUNE: Roses

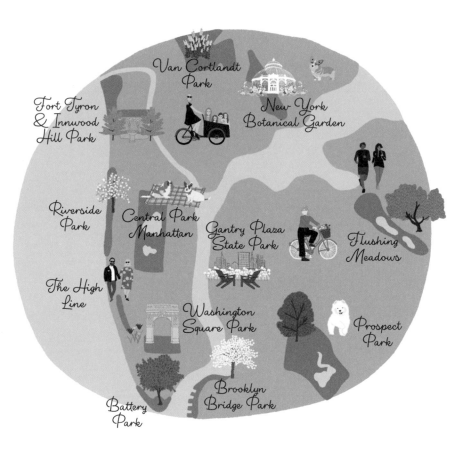

Van Cortlandt Park

New York Botanical Garden

Fort Tyron & Innwood Hill Park

Riverside Park

Central Park Manhattan

Gantry Plaza State Park

Flushing Meadows

The High Line

Washington Square Park

Prospect Park

Battery Park

Brooklyn Bridge Park

NYC PARKS

New York's parks serve so many purposes – meeting places, playgrounds, *gardens* and woodlands – and they all offer an escape from the cacophony and hustle of the city. On warm days the parks will be filled with people *picnicking*, kids playing and friends catching up. In the colder seasons you'll find people bundled up, enjoying the winter *scenery* and fresh air. These beautiful parks dotted around New York offer up *nature and calm*, serving locals and visitors alike. No visit to New York is complete without appreciating the *beautiful* green spaces.

Central Park
Manhattan
Museums, theatres, scenic views, a zoo, formal gardens, woodlands, bird watching . . . and so much more.

Battery Park
Financial District, 10004
Statue of Liberty views, memorials, museums and waterfront walkways.

Brooklyn Bridge Park
Brooklyn, 11201
Downtown views and ample green space to enjoy.

Flushing Meadows
Queens, 11368
Museums, World's Fair monuments, playgrounds and a zoo.

Fort Tyron & Innwood Hill Park
Washington Heights, 10040
Hudson views, beautiful gardens and the Met Cloisters.

Gantry Plaza State Park
Queens, 10007
Stunning Midtown and East River views.

The High Line
Chelsea, 10011
Raised garden path with lovely views and a vast selection of foliage.

New York Botanical Garden

The Bronx, 10458

Sprawling botanical garden with every type of plant you can imagine.

Prospect Park

Brooklyn, 11225

Charming boathouse, zoo, woodlands and Brooklyn Botanic Garden.

Riverside Park

Upper West Side

East River views, inventive playgrounds, memorials and scenic paths.

Van Cortlandt Park

The Bronx, 10471

Visit the Van Cortlandt House Museum, walking trails and freshwater lake.

Washington Square Park

Greenwich Village, 10012

Historic park with beautiful trees and lots of benches to sit and enjoy the atmosphere.

Ladurée

The Carlyle

Peak Restaurant & Bar

BG Restaurant

Grand Central Oyster Bar

abc Kitchen & abcV

One If By Land, Two If By Sea

Minetta Tavern

Union Square Cafe

Manhatta

The Fulton

The River Cafe

CELEBRATING IN NYC

NEW YORK BY SEASON

Celebrating milestones, achievements and
accolades is one of the *great joys* of life. One
of my favourite ways to mark an occasion is a
memorable meal, and New York has no shortage
of amazing places that will make any
celebration one to remember.

VIEWS

The Fulton by Jean-Georges
89 South St, Financial District, 10038
Boasting Brooklyn Bridge views and freshly caught fish, this is a great place to celebrate.

Manhatta
60th Floor, 28 Liberty St, Financial District, 10005
Elegant dining and stunning views combine to make this restaurant a great choice for a special occasion.

Peak Restaurant & Bar
101st Floor, 30 Hudson Yards, Chelsea, 10001
Breathtaking views of New York and top-notch food served on the 101st floor of Hudson Yards.

The River Cafe
1 Water St, Brooklyn, 11201
Tucked just next to Brooklyn Bridge, this restaurant has unrivalled river views, great food and a charming atmosphere.

AFTERNOON TEA

BG Restaurant
7th Floor, 754 5th Ave, Upper East Side, 10019
Serving afternoon tea and Central Park views, this Bergdorf Goodman restaurant is perfect for a special occasion.

The Carlyle
35 E 76th St, Upper East Side, 10021
An opulent choice for cabaret-style dinner at Cafe Carlyle, or an exquisite afternoon tea in The Gallery.

Ladurée
Various locations, SoHo, Upper East Side
Enjoy a delicious afternoon tea or patisseries in the NY outposts of the classic French macaroon shop.

NEW YORK BY SEASON

DINNER

abc Kitchen & abcV
38 E 19th St, Midtown, 10003
Farm fresh menu served in a wonderful atmosphere. You can enjoy an entirely vegan menu at abcV and both restaurants are equally delicious.

Minetta Tavern
113 MacDougal St, Greenwich Village, 10012
A cosy French bistro with snug corners and classic French faire. A good choice for a relaxed environment.

One If By Land, Two If By Sea
17 Barrow St, West Village, 10014
A prix fixe menu and a romantic atmosphere in this historic carriage house once owned by Aaron Burr.

Union Square Cafe
101 E 19th St, Union Sq, 10003
Wonderful ambiance and great food that focuses on local, fresh ingredients.

Grand Central Oyster Bar
89 E 42nd St, Midtown, 10017
For over a century this restaurant has been feeding travellers and locals. With an expansive selection of oysters and daily specials, its seafood selection can't be beat.

The Cloisters and Fort Tryon Park

New York Botanical Garden

Pelham Bay Park

Riverside Park

Central Park

Roosevelt Island

Greenbelt Nature Center

Prospect Park

Farmers' Markets

Brooklyn Botanical Gardens

Clove Lakes Park

NYC IN AUTUMN

NEW YORK BY SEASON

Autumn is one of the best times to visit New York. The weather is cooler but not too cold, the fall foliage in the parks and green spaces is *spectacular*; homes and shops are *decorated* with fall decor, and autumnal treats and drinks abound. If you are wanting to *embrace autumn,* here are the best places to explore.

Central Park

Manhattan

In the fall the leaves in Central Park turn beautiful colours. You can enjoy especially spectacular foliage near the boathouse.

The Cloisters and Fort Tryon Park

Washington Heights, 10040

These riverside parks have vibrant leaves set against the Hudson River.

Clove Lakes Park

1150 Clove Rd, Staten Island, 10301

Beautiful fall foliage can be found, especially around the lake; it's the perfect place to take a stroll.

Farmers' Markets

Multiple locations, Union Square, Chelsea, Tompkins Square, Fort Greene, Park Slope

One fall treat that you must try is warm apple cider with an apple cider doughnut. Available at weekend farmers' markets, it is worth seeking them out.

Greenbelt Nature Center

700 Rockland Ave, Staten Island, 10341

This Staten Island green space offers up hiking paths and trails, and you'll find yourself surrounded in autumnal colours.

New York and Brooklyn Botanical Gardens
The Bronx, Brooklyn
From fall foliage to flowers, the botanical gardens are
beautiful in this season.

Pelham Bay Park
Middletown Rd & Stadium Ave, The Bronx, 10465
Vast park with trails and forests, making it an autumnal foliage paradise.

Prospect Park
Brooklyn
With ample tree-lined paths and walkways, this park becomes
vibrant in the autumn and is a great place to see the leaves.

Riverside Park
Upper West Side
Lovely tree-lined paths with leaves in every colour.

Roosevelt Island
East River, 10044
The Smallpox Memorial Hospital's vine-covered walls turn red
and orange, making this ruined building a sight to behold.

New Year's Eve

Thanksgiving

Halloween

Independence Day

HOLIDAYS IN NYC

NEW YORK BY SEASON

If you happen to be in NY for a holiday, you are in for a treat. The city *loves* a holiday and goes all out. From decorations to festivities, there are countless ways to enjoy a *holiday celebration* in the city. While some holidays only have festivities on that day, others have events in the weeks leading up to the holiday, so can be *enjoyed* all season.

Halloween

October 31st

Halloween is a very popular holiday in NYC. Houses get spooky decorations, pumpkins line the doorsteps and there are lots of festive events as well. To see spooky décor, head to the residential areas of the West Village, Upper West Side and Upper East Side. For Halloween-themed events, check out Green-Wood Cemetery, the Village Halloween Parade or the annual Halloween Pumpkin Flotilla in Central Park.

Independence Day

July 4th

The 4th of July is a national holiday in the USA, and lots of businesses are closed, but it is still a great time to visit the city. They have one of the biggest fireworks displays in the world to celebrate the day. The Macy's Fourth of July fireworks launch from barges in the East River and can be viewed on either the Manhattan side or the Brooklyn side.

New Year's Eve
December 31st

New York has one of the most iconic ways to
ring in the new year with its annual Ball Drop in
Times Square. There is always an epic show and
fireworks display, but keep in mind it can get
very crowded and is usually very cold. Liberty
Island also has a New Year fireworks display with
the backdrop of the Statue of Liberty. Another
way to view the fireworks is from a harbour
cruise, which positions you perfectly to enjoy
the display throughout the city.

Thanksgiving
Fourth Thursday in November

Thanksgiving is a national holiday, and many businesses
will be closed, but you can celebrate by watching the Macy's
Thanksgiving Day Parade. This annual tradition has been taking
place for the past 100 years. You can line the parade route and
watch it or opt to watch it on TV. In the lead-up to Thanksgiving,
bakeries, grocery shops and food stores will have special
Thanksgiving treats. Pie is a big part of the holiday, and you will
find pumpkin pie, pecan pie, apple pie, cherry pie and more on
many dessert counters throughout the city.

Daily
Provisions

Max Brenner
Chocolate Bar

Levain

Bar
Pisellino

Schmackary's

Angelina
Paris

Dominique
Ansel
Bakery

L. A.
Burdick

Lafayette Grand
Cafe & Bakery

Milk Bar

MarieBelle

Ferrara
Bakery &
Cafe

Doughnut
Plant

Four & Twenty
Blackbirds

NYC WINTER TREATS

NEW YORK BY SEASON

Delicious winter treats and warming drinks are the *perfect remedy* for cold winter New York days. As winter settles in, bakeries and cafes offer up *seasonal delights* with flavours of peppermint, gingerbread and *cinnamon* wafting through the air. It can easily be agreed that the holiday season is best enjoyed with a *cosy drink* in hand.

Angelina Paris
Bryant Park 1050 6th Ave,
Midtown, 10018
Richly luxurious hot chocolate.

Bar Pisellino
52 Grove St, Greenwich Village, 10014
Thick and delicious Italian-style hot chocolate.

Daily Provisions
Multiple locations, Upper West Side, Union Square, West Village
Gingerbread peppermint cruller.

Dominique Ansel Bakery
189 Spring St, SoHo, 10012
Santa religieuse, blooming hot chocolate and chocolate pinecone.

Doughnut Plant
Multiple Locations Across NYC
Holiday doughnuts, including the gingerbread man and marzipan star.

Ferrara Bakery & Cafe
195 Grand St, Little Italy, 10013
Enjoy the struffoli, a classic Italian Christmas dessert.

Four & Twenty Blackbirds
Multiple locations in Brooklyn, Park Slope and Prospect Heights
Chocolate-orange almond pie.

L. A. Burdick
156 Prince St, SoHo, 10012
Single-origin hot cocoa and handmade chocolates.

Lafayette Grand Cafe & Bakery
380 Lafayette St, NoHo, 10003
Christmas wheel pastry.

Levain
Multiple locations, Upper West Side, NoHo, Upper East Side, Harlem, Brooklyn
Dark-chocolate peppermint cookie.

MarieBelle
484 Broome St, SoHo, 10013
Decadent hot cocoa in a handful of delicious flavours.

Max Brenner Chocolate Bar
841 Broadway, Union Square, 10003
Tasty hot chocolate that is sure to please.

Milk Bar
Multiple locations
Peppermint-cornflake-chocolate-chip cookies.

Schmackary's
362 W 45th St, Midtown, 10036
The dirty peppermint cookie.

See The
Nutcracker

See the
Decorations

Christmas Market

See the
Lights

Go Ice
Skating

Go to a Christmas
Show

CHRISTMAS IN NYC

New York goes all out when it comes to Christmas. From *twinkling lights* to shops and homes decked out, the city is a magical place to experience the Christmas season. The cold weather and chance of snow make *winter festivities* all the more enjoyable. 'Tis the season to bundle up with a thick coat and warm boots and enjoy the city as the lights *twinkle* in the evening, keeping warm by enjoying a hot cocoa and listening to the *festive music* playing in all the stores. It truly is the most *magical* time of the year.

TIPS FOR EXPLORING NEW YORK

I hope you find inspiration in these illustrations. New York has been a thriving city for hundreds of years and there will always be something more to explore. There is no 'right' way to explore New York; the perfect trip is the trip that involves doing things that you value when travelling. If you love food, make sure you plan for amazing meals. If you love a good view, make sure you see New York from all the best heights.

Here are things to think about to ensure you get the best from the city, whether you are visiting or are a born-and-bred New Yorker.

1. What is important to you when you take a holiday? Are you looking to relax? Explore neighbourhoods like a local? Eat at Michelin-star restaurants? Whatever the answer to this question is, make sure you prioritize that for your trip.

2. Wear practical shoes. New York is very walkable, and you can easily find yourself walking 20k+ steps a day. New Yorkers are practical people, so wear practical shoes.

3. Take time to enjoy the atmosphere. Make sure you sometimes put your phone and camera down and just enjoy the views and sites.

4. Don't stand in the middle of the sidewalk to check your phone.

5. Book restaurants in advance when you can.

6. Don't try to do everything. Pick a few things and do them well; you won't be disappointed.